LETTERS OF ANDREW JUKES

LETTERS OF

ANDREW JUKES

EDITED WITH A BIOGRAPHICAL

By HERBERT H. JEAFFRESON

Vicar of The Grange, Bishop Auckland,
and late Chaplain to the Bishop of Durham

WITH PHOTOGRAVURE PORTRAIT

LONGMANS, GREEN, AND CO
39 PATERNOSTER ROW, LONDON
NEW YORK AND BOMBAY
1903

LETTERS OF
ANDREW JUKES

EDITED, WITH A SHORT BIOGRAPHY,

By *HERBERT H. JEAFFRESON*

Author of 'The Divine Unity and Trinity'
'The Church of the Living God' &c.

WITH PHOTOGRAVURE PORTRAIT

LONGMANS, GREEN, AND CO.
39 PATERNOSTER ROW, LONDON
NEW YORK AND BOMBAY
1903

than I the records of his life at Hull. But the natural course of time makes those friends few, and there is probably no one who could be invited to undertake a task which, with all my defects, I am thankful to perform.

Some of his friends (to whom I offer my hearty thanks) have most kindly put into my hands letters which they have preserved. To these have been added a great number of copies or first draughts of letters which Mr. Jukes himself preserved. Though a copious and ready writer, he took great pains to insure the clear expression of his thoughts. The total number of letters which have been entrusted to me is about one thousand.

The work of selection has not been light. Almost all the letters which have reached me have dealt with important topics, and very few are without striking passages. At the same time, in many of them there is so much repetition that it was impossible to print them all. My principle of selection has been to choose those letters which deal with important subjects in the clearest language; and not to exclude letters because they were less in accordance with my own convictions.

Few of the letters are printed quite *in extenso*. Whenever omissions have been made, the place is invariably marked by a row of points, with the one exception that references to chapter and verse in Holy Scripture are sometimes left out as superfluous. In the very few cases in which it was necessary to supply a word, the insertion has been marked by square brackets. I have taken considerable liberty with the punctuation, which (as is frequently the case in letters) was often capricious and perplexing.

It has seemed wise to print the letters not according to their topics but in chronological order. In some respects the writer's mind passed through so great a development that it would be unfair to omit a clear indication of the date at which he was writing.

With a very few exceptions, I have decided to omit the names of Mr. Jukes's correspondents. Some of them requested this course ; some of the letters of which the writer kept copies are without names; and in other cases it did not seem fair to print the name of the recipient of the letter without obtaining his sanction. For similar reasons, names which occur in the body of a letter have been concealed under false initials.

In order that the reader may understand the various phases through which Mr. Jukes's mind passed it has seemed desirable to prefix to his letters a short account of his life. There were not, indeed, sufficient events of importance to justify a long biography; nor do I flatter myself with the supposition that I possess the gifts which make biography interesting. I have made no attempt at drawing or criticising the character of my friend; I have not attempted to estimate or to harmonise his opinions. Those opinions the reader will find in his letters or in his books. The character of Mr. Jukes was not that of a consistent and systematic philosopher, but that of a seer, whose eyes were opened to discern what most men ignore. It is likely that every reader will find in these letters points on which he will think the writer mistaken; but I shall be greatly disappointed if people do not find in them fresh indications of the mind of God, and impulses to seek for that truth which he who seeks finds.

H. H. J.

CONTENTS

LIFE OF ANDREW JUKES

THE family of Jukes resided in ancient times in Cumberland. Thence, early in the fourteenth century, one Sidward Jukes migrated to Shropshire and Staffordshire, in which counties his descendants have continued to live.

A member of this family, Andrew, who was born in 1776, married in 1814 a daughter of John Ewart, Inspector of Hospitals in India, whose wife was the second daughter of Ephraim Lopez Pereira, Baron d'Aguilar. Andrew Jukes took his bride to Bombay, where he practised medicine; but being employed by the East India Company as an envoy to the Court of Persia, he died at Ispahan, November 21, 1821, and is buried in the Armenian cemetery outside that city.

His eldest child, Andrew John, was born at Bombay, November 5, 1815. He always remembered with pleasure that the day of his birth was the day on which the news of the battle of Waterloo reached Bombay.

His grandmother, Mrs. Ewart, had accompanied her daughter to India ; and in 1820 she brought the little Andrew and his brother Mark home to England. Leaving the children under the care of their father's sister, Mrs. Worthington, of Moorhill House, Stourport, Worcestershire, Mrs. Ewart returned to India, where she found her daughter a widow; and in 1822 she brought her and her younger children, Laura and Augustus, to England.

For his grandmother, Mrs. Ewart, Mr. Jukes always had a deep love and veneration. To her apparently he owed his first instruction in the Gospel of Christ. When, at the age of twelve, he went to school at Harrow, Mrs. Ewart went to reside there in order to provide him with a home. A letter written by him to the Rev. and Hon. Canon Bridgman in 1890 gives some details of his school life.

I went to Harrow in the October quarter of 1827, the same day with Frederick William Faber, when we and John Merivale were all three placed together at the bottom of the Third Remove of the Fourth Form. The next quarter saw us all at the top of the Remove. From that time till I left Harrow, we three always sat together in class, first one and then another being at the top. Faber first boarded at Dr. Butler's ; but when Dr. Longley came, in

April 1829, Faber removed to Mr. Mills's house, where I also boarded with him, though when I first entered the school I was a home-boarder. After he took his degree at Oxford, where he was Fellow of University, Faber, as you probably know, went over to Rome, and became an Oratorian. . . . After my leaving Harrow at midsummer, 1832, I went into the army for three years, which made me a year or two later at Cambridge than the other boys who were at Harrow with me. . . . But Robert Broughton, and his brother Henry, now of St. Mary's, Leicester, were Cambridge men—the latter one of my closest friends there, and ever since.

What a flood of boyish memories those old names bring back to me! 'All the burial-places of memory give up their dead.' Faber, whom perhaps I knew as well as any one at Harrow, was a remarkable boy. He was the only boy in my time who stayed for Holy Communion.[1] I remember how he used (partly, I think, to perplex old Mills, with whom we boarded) to go down after the eight o'clock evening prayers in the house to Mills's study, and bore him with questions as to something in Sophocles or Aristophanes, which we might then be reading. . . . N. was one who often amused the school. After one of the holidays, when we were in the Sixth Form, he came back to Harrow in a wig. During the holidays he had, either for a fancy ball or for some private theatricals, had his head shaved to represent some character—if I remember right, he had appeared as the devil. His wig in school caused great amusement. Sometimes in construing, when he stuck at a word, he would pull the wig away or push it off, and cause a titter round the class. . . . If you care

---

[1] Andrew Jukes was himself a communicant at Harrow.

a

to go into the old school-room, you may see my name
cut, just behind where I used to sit when I was in the
Second Remove of the Fourth Form, at the south-west
corner of the room, on the west wall.   Faber's name,
I think, is cut larger on the opposite side.

On leaving school, in 1832, Andrew Jukes received a commission in the army of the Hon. East
India Company, and was sent to Poona, whither his
grandmother followed him.   To the end of his life
his gait bore witness to his military training, and he
traced a nobler lesson to that source.   'As a youth,'
he writes in 1862 to a friend who seemed to him dis-
ingenuous, 'I was trained in a school—as a soldier,
I mean—where to speak the truth without equivoca-
tion was almost the only virtue thought of.'   We
may conjecture that the reason of his retirement
from the army was the deepening of his desire to
serve God in the sacred ministry.   'Quite in my
early years,' he writes, 'I was awakened to desire to
live for God;' but in several letters he refers to a
time of more decided conversion, which in an inscrip-
tion in a copy of Scott's Bible he ascribes to the
reading of that work when in hospital in India.   In
1837 he returned to England, and the following year
he entered at Trinity College, Cambridge.   There it
was his 'daily practice' to study the Bible in his

rooms; and he was one of the undergraduates who taught in the well-known Jesus Lane Sunday-schools. He was too late to come under the personal influence of Charles Simeon, who died in 1836. He speaks of the help he received from Professor Corrie in the study, mainly historical, of the Prayer Book; and he has spoken of kindnesses rendered by J. B. Jukes, the geologist, with whom, however, he could claim no kinship. In 1840 he won the Hulsean Prize with an essay on 'The Principles of Prophetic Interpretation.'

About that date he met and became attached to Augusta, the third daughter of Admiral Hole, a distinguished officer, who, after serving at Trafalgar, had settled at Barnstaple. As Mr. Jukes had offered himself to the Church Missionary Society for service at Sierra Leone, Admiral Hole at first refused his sanction to a marriage which would carry his daughter to so unhealthy a station. But the plan of missionary work fell through, chiefly because Mr. Jukes felt it a duty to provide a home for Mrs. Ewart; and the marriage took place on January 27, 1842. Mrs. Ewart accompanied the young pair to their new home, and remained with them until her death, at the age of ninety-two, in 1852.

It would be presumptuous if the present writer

were to attempt to describe Mrs. Jukes's character, the more because his knowledge of her extended over only the last six years of her life; but he recalls with affectionate veneration the sweet and gracious gravity of her careworn face as she would sit almost silent while her husband opened the mysteries of God, kindling at once when there was an opportunity of helping anyone. She was one who had learned prudence as well as love in the school of Christ.; and many beside her children will rise and call her blessed.

On the second Sunday after Trinity, June 12, 1842, he was ordained Deacon by the Archbishop of York in his cathedral, and was licensed to the curacy of St. John's Church, Hull, of which the Rev. Thomas Dykes was Vicar. He passed so good an examination that the Archbishop not only exempted him from the usual examination for the Priesthood, but nominated him as preacher at the ordination in the following year, when he should be raised to that degree.

But a very different course lay before him. The time was one of intense excitement in the English Church. The storm which arose about the ' Tracts for the Times' was at its height. Bishops, politicians, journalists were raging against the Oxford theologians ; and the earlier secessions to Rome among

Newman's followers had begun. Mr. Jukes had not
been to any considerable extent influenced by the
Oxford Movement; though he already sympathised
with its protest against the blasphemous Erastianism ·
which made the Royal Supremacy a cloak for the
tyranny of Parliament over the Church. He admired
also the devotion and zeal for good works which
were shown by the Tractarian leaders.

I shall never forget (he writes many years later) my
first reading of Dr. Pusey's first tract, in the ' Tracts for
the Times,' on Fasting. In my poor way I had always
tried to practise abstinence, but Pusey's tract gave me
direction and encouragement; for the good Pharisees
among whom I then was cast had improved upon the old
Pharisee's prayer, and while they yet said, ' God, I thank
Thee that I am not as other men,' they concluded by saying,
' I do *not* fast at all; I do *not* gives tithe of all that
I possess.' What a change has come over the Church
since then ! It has been like spring-time after frost.

But he had not emerged from the tradition of his
childhood, which identified regeneration with conversion ; and probably the obligation which his office
laid upon him of declaring that the baptised child
is regenerate forced on his conscience the plain sense
of words which in his study had seemed less cogent
and less obnoxious. Nor was the language of the
Baptismal Service the only difficulty which he found

self-made prophets, the strifes and separations which followed. Gradually I learnt that one cannot act upon a mere *direction* of Scripture without *power*, and that the assumption of power may be a great pretence. . . . For a fallen Church, or for a section of it, to attempt or pretend to take the ground or do the work of the Church in Apostolic days was about as absurd as to pretend to make an old man young.

In doctrine, then, and in practice Mr. Jukes and his followers resembled the Plymouth Brethren, a sect then about fourteen years old, which had for its distinctive mark the eschewing of all that was thought formal in religion, especially a stated ministry, and constant dependence on the inspiration of the Holy Ghost. We do not find, however, any indication that Mr. Jukes followed the Plymouth Brethren in another of their characteristics, the 'Breaking of Bread' every Lord's Day. It is hardly surprising that Mr. Jukes and his wife submitted to rebaptism at the hands of Mr. Daniell, a Baptist minister. Few letters survive, or at least few have reached the present writer, which deal in detail with the difficulties and disappointments to which the letter last quoted refers. In some of those which have been preserved there may be noticed a tone of asperity and assertion of his own judgment which is strange to those who knew the writer at a later time, when gentleness and largeness of mind were among his most conspicuous qualities. Meanwhile, he was constantly studying the Bible and the Fathers, and mystical writers such as Boehme and Law; and at one time he was in frequent correspondence with Frederick Denison Maurice. In 1847 the first of his longer books appeared, 'The Law of the Offerings in Leviticus.' The substance of this book had been delivered in the form of lectures to his congregation. When the author was about to print his notes with corrections he received a letter from one of his hearers, who told him that he had taken down the lectures in shorthand and intended to publish them. The law of copyright gave the author no protection for sermons which had been preached; and Mr. Jukes had to purchase his own work for one hundred pounds. The thesis of the book is that the different sorts of sacrifice in the Old Law represent different aspects of the Sacrifice of Christ, and that the varieties of each sort of sacrifice typify the degrees in which different believers apprehend His work. In later years Mr. Jukes used to speak of this book as immature, and at one time he was disposed to revise it and enlarge it, especially with regard to the perpetuation of the Sacrifice of Christ in the Holy Eucharist and in the life of the believer. His next work was on the 'Characteristic Differences of the Four Gospels,' a less original and less interesting work, perhaps, but notable as displaying a much greater familiarity with the Fathers. His advance in this study was still more fully shown in the 'Types of Genesis.'

Meanwhile, the congregation, which had passed from the street into a room, found its place too strait for it, and it was proposed to build a chapel. The events are narrated in a letter of 1864.

My difficulty is not so much about a chapel as whether, having gathered so many poor souls here, I am justified in leaving them. I can say from my heart that personally I have not the slightest wish to have a chapel. I rather shrink from it, knowing what the state of the Church is at this time, and fearing lest, if a chapel were built, it would only be a scene of failure. At the same time, seeing I could not gather the souls whom the Lord had given me in our present room, I was willing to make an appeal to friends as to a chapel, desiring to accept the response they made as an indication of what the Lord's will might be respecting me. The result of my appeal to brethren was that I got nearly enough to buy the ground for a chapel; and for three years nothing more was sent me. Hence I concluded that it was the Lord's will I should not go on with the work; and this, with other circumstances, led me to think my work in Hull was done. I therefore make some arrangements about moving to London; and then, just as I was about to go, the love of the poor souls here presses them to offer me nearly all they have if only I will stay and still minister among them. They have within the last fortnight or three weeks promised quite half of what a chapel would cost; and if I will stay they will work to raise the rest. But the question on my mind is this, Is this after all the Lord's will? Has not the Lord rather seemed to show, by denying me a chapel for so many years, that it is not His will that I should serve in this manner? And might I not really serve Him, and serve His scattered children, better by writing than by making another sect, or even another congregation? My experience of what brethren are in these days; the trial, too, of watching for them—the frost by night and the drought by day, as Jacob said—and the grief, constantly recurring, of seeing some of them torn by wild beasts; my failing strength and spirits, too—all these have seemed to say, Do not attempt a new chapel; while, on the other hand, there is the cry of all the poor brethren here, Do stay and work with us, and build a chapel to gather us. So I am dragged hither and thither, nor do I know anyone who seems able to say a single word of advice one way or another. . . . You can, however, serve me by praying for me; and I have no doubt that, through God's grace, I shall, even if I miss my way, have my error overruled to God's glory.

The chapel was built, a beautiful little cruciform structure, holding some six hundred persons, and was dedicated in the summer of 1866 to the service of Almighty God under the title of the Church of St. John the Evangelist. It is significant of the change that had passed over Mr. Jukes's views that some of his more extreme friends among the Plymouth

Brethren felt themselves unable to attend the dedication when they knew that he intended to use the
Church service; for they feared that in 'going down
into the stream to reach others, he himself might be
swept away.'   A Protestant newspaper commented
sarcastically on the combination of 'Ritualistic services'
and a Baptist chapel, though indeed the 'Ritualism'
went no further than a hymn translated from the
Breviary, and the use of the surplice in the pulpit.
It is worth notice that he prepared a Hymnal for his
congregation, which, though for the most part intensely
subjective in tone, provided hymns for the Christian
seasons, and for the festivals of saints.   'He hoped,'
writes one who knew him most intimately, 'his
people would follow him, but comparatively few did
so: the congregation was a new one.'

But another cause was about to put an end to Mr.
Jukes's life at Hull.   An old friend of his, who had
long been in the habit of consulting him about
difficulties of faith, was perplexed by the popular
doctrine as to everlasting punishment.   The subject
was by no means a new one to Mr. Jukes.   He
gives an account of the growth of his thought in
an essay in the 'Literary Churchman,' March 20,
1891. Even as an undergraduate he had been
impressed by the fact that, in the Old Testament,

many ordinances and judgments are said to be 'eternal' which nevertheless came to an end. Thence he gathered that 'eternal' and 'everlasting' are not interchangeable terms. He passed on to the consideration that the work of God is carried on in successive 'ages' or 'eternities.' He had, further, learned that God does not save us from death but by death, so that the expression 'the second death' suggests that this, like the first death, is part of the scheme of the redemption of man from a world of sin. And, finally, his attention was called to God's method of saving an election that through it He may save the whole body ; and that the Christian Church, being an elect few, was chosen not only to inherit a blessing but also to convey that blessing to the non-elect. These views he expounded in a series of letters to his friend. The work was circulated in manuscript among a few persons ; but for a long time he refused to publish it, not doubting its truth, but doubting whether the truth was one which was fitted to those times. Finally, he submitted the letters to certain persons in whose judgment he had confidence, and by their advice published them in 1867 under the title of ' The Second Death and the Restitution of All Things.' With none other of his works did he take so much care, revising it diligently for successive editions, and especially adding evidence that the hope which he advocated had been held and sanctioned in the early ages of the Church.

The publication of this book led to bitter controversy. Many of his old associates held strongly the doctrine of endless pain ; more, perhaps, were in favour of the doctrine of the annihilation of the wicked. Both sections assailed him with vigour, and perhaps with acrimony ; nor can we deny that in Mr. Jukes's own letters there is a tone of asperity. He seems to be surprised that the truth which had commended itself to him should not meet with instant acceptance at the hands of others. His letters at this period are plainly the words of one who was overstrained and in a state of nervous irritability. He had passed through twenty-five years of spiritual tension. He had borne the care of many souls who looked to him for guidance, and had learned what an exhaustive test of love it is to lay down life for friends. He had suffered the disappointment of an idealist who finds that the material with which he works does not accomplish his ideal. His own views had been greatly modified. On the appointment in 1860 of his old schoolmaster, Dr. Longley, to the See of York, he had been urged to return to the English Church, to be ordained Priest, and to accept the care of a parish ; and the inability to accept his invitation caused him almost as much distress as his first secession. The strain of collecting money for the building of a chapel must have been burdensome to one who was never a man of business. He had adopted in the chapel the Church service, believing it would serve his flock, but they refused to follow him. And now, those with whom he had been in sympathy rejected him as one who denied the faith of Christ for which he gave his soul, and refused for themselves the doctrine which he conceived to be the vindication of the love of God and the hope of the anxious believer. Who can wonder that, under so complicated a strain, his bodily and mental health broke down, and that there are signs of his collapse in the irritable tone of his letters ? Many years before, he had been thrown from his horse, and the skull had been indented, causing pressure on the brain which at times gave rise to acute pain, and to some of the symptoms of paralysis. In this condition of broken health he left Hull, never expecting to resume his work, and in the winter of 1867–8 he took a long tour in Greece, Egypt, and the Holy Land. The chapel was sold to a congregation of Presbyterians.

From the tour he returned in better health, but still unfit for work. He was at this time only in his

b

fifty-third year. In April 1868 he left Hull; and after spending a year at Bridlington, in March 1869 he moved to Highgate, in order to be near his younger son, who, as a solicitor, was required to spend a year in London.

The change was in much more than locality. He had resolved to seek restoration to the ministry of the English Church; and the earliest letter from Highgate which is preserved is one which he addressed to the Bishop of London (Jackson) on this subject. It is mainly concerned with the correction of a vague charge which had reached the Bishop, that he had been unsound with respect to the Holy Trinity. Whether he sought for ordination to the Priesthood or not, we are not able to say. He never became a Priest; but he received from the Bishop of London (as afterwards from the Bishop of Rochester) permission to officiate. The time, indeed, was not yet come for him to act on this permission, for he was still in very infirm health, suffering from pain and giddiness in the head and from numbness in the side. He attended some religious meetings, and began to hold Bible readings in his house. In time he recovered the power of preaching occasionally without injury, and, indeed, he felt himself refreshed by proclaiming again the Gospel which was his life.

And he speaks with thankfulness, in 1871, of having been able to write three letters to the ' Guardian ' on the subject of Restitution.

We have seen that, during his life at Hull, he had been a diligent student of Holy Scripture and of the Fathers. From these sources he had gradually learned to modify the theological views with which he began life. He had come to see the reality of sacramental grace, which, indeed, is implied in the conviction, so strong in his mind, that our salvation is to be traced rather to what Christ is than to what He has done. But at Hull Mr. Jukes probably had but few opportunities of coming into contact with the Catholic revival, which, starting from Oxford, had been permeating the English Church, but was perhaps less operative in the North than in the South. He had, indeed, some friendly intercourse with Archdeacon Robert Isaac Wilberforce, the most intellectual and learned member of a remarkable family ; but this intercourse had been interrupted by the secession of Wilberforce to the Roman Church, and his death, which quickly followed. In London, Mr. Jukes came to form friendships with many men who were in a greater or less degree associated with this movement. His elder son became Curate to the venerable Rector of Clewer, and with him, as with

Mr. Hutchings, then Chaplain of the House of Mercy,
and now Archdeacon of Cleveland, Mr. Jukes was on
terms of mutual affection and respect. About 1870
he was visited by Mr. and Mrs. Pearsall Smith, who
came from America with the purpose of holding
religious meetings; and through them he became
acquainted with Mr. and Mrs. Cowper Temple
(afterwards Lord and Lady Mount Temple), at whose
houses he met many men of schools from which he
had stood aloof. It was the charitable design of Mr.
and Mrs. Cowper Temple to gather together at their
houses in Great Stanhope Street, and at Broadlands
near Romsey, men of various ecclesiastical positions
and tempers, who were agreed in love for our
Saviour. These meetings grew into the well-known
Broadlands Conferences, the first of which was held
in 1871. At these there was not a little to justify
the good-humoured description of a writer in the
'Pilot,' October 26, 1901 :

> The debate was animated, amiable, and desultory. No
> one kept to the prescribed subject. Everyone had his own
> gospel, and preached it. Everyone agreed immensely with
> the last speaker, and forthwith proceeded to launch some
> entirely novel theory of his own. There was no quarrelling,
> and the mutual admiration was perfectly sincere.

But a more adequate estimate of the meetings may

be drawn from letters written by Mr. Jukes in 1879
and 1875 respectively :

The Broadlands meeting this year was a very remarkable
one.   We reaped to the end what dear George Body sowed
at the beginning.   There were one or two little incidents
which would have made you frown and smile.   One dear very
Evangelical soul who was present thought it his duty to tell
Z., after one of his most beautiful addresses, that he (Z.)
was not converted.   Z.'s reply was like himself, ' Well,
then, it must be a beautiful thing to be converted ; for if
the sight of the Blessed Lord gives such joy to a poor unconverted soul like me, what must He be to us when we
are indeed converted ! '   P.'s answer, too, to L. (when the
latter, wishing to prepare P. for any Ritualistic forms at
the Abbey, told him that he must not be surprised if Mr.
N., in celebrating the Holy Communion, made several bow-
ings or genuflections) was beautiful : ' Don't say a word
to me about that : I have seen Christ in that man (N.),
and that is enough for me.'

Shall I tell you what I thought I heard after I left your
door ?   I had just taken my seat in the carriage, and was
lifting up my heart for a blessing on the house which we
were leaving, when all through the park, as I sat silent
with closed eyes, I heard, or seemed to hear, now rising, now
falling, one reiterated strain of grand and stately music,
and all through it just two words, and only two, came to
my ears—' Praise Him, praise Him, praise Him '—till we
had passed your lodge gates.

About this time I made the acquaintance of
Mr. Jukes, and I cannot deny myself the pleasure of
narrating the beginning of a friendship which has

been among the chief blessings of my life. In the autumn of 1873 I was appointed to a curacy at High-gate, and the priest under whom I worked introduced me to a clergyman whom he described as a man ' mighty in the Scriptures.' He was a tall man, with a military gait, his long beard already grey, his eyes of that clear blue colour which seems proper to seers. A few days later, Mr. Jukes called upon me, and I returned his call. For a time our conversation flagged, until mention chanced to be made of a recent translation of Origen. 'Do you love Origen?' said Mr. Jukes ; 'then we must be friends.' And a true friend he proved himself. It came to be our habit to take long walks together, during which he would talk over any subject he had in mind, and teach me still more by the Socratic method of drawing out my thoughts, helping me to see their defects, and leaving me with materials for a wiser judgment. After a lapse of more than a quarter of a century, I am not more impressed by the recollection of my own crudities than by the patient humility with which he would listen to them. It is characteristic of him that for a year at least he never spoke to me on the subject of Restitution, thinking that I ' had enough on hand without it. There is a time for everything.' Perhaps for the same reason he never spoke to me of the

Bible-readings which he held at his house. Sometimes he would preach for us at All Saints' Church,
though he would say that his days for preaching were
over. His preaching was a practical exposition of
the words spoken about our Lord, that 'He spake as
One having authority, and not as the scribes.' He was
very simple, he used much repetition, he did not shrink
from the most familiar illustrations. 'We talk about
our dear Lord,' he would say ; 'what does *dear* mean ?
When we say that a cabbage is dear, we mean that we
give much for it. Our Lord is dear if we give much
for Him.' He sometimes caused a smile. But he
always spoke as one who saw the truth which he was
describing, and did not report it on the authority of
others. He was always present at the early celebra-
tions of Holy Communion. The first time I had the
privilege of worshipping by his side was at the Holy
Eucharist at St. Barnabas', Pimlico, when his devotion
made me think of St. John when heaven was opened
to him. That church was destined to be for him and
for myself the place of much blessed worship. In
1877 he returned from Broadlands full of the beauty
of face and character of a young priest, Alfred Gurney,
then at Brighton, who in the following year was
appointed Vicar of St. Barnabas'. To Alfred Gurney
should have come the task of editing the letters of

him whom we revered and loved as our master in
Christ; but he was called early to his rest in 1898,
and left the work to incompetent hands.

In 1879, Mrs. Jukes's health, which had long been
infirm, rendered necessary a removal from Highgate,
and a house was taken on a hill above Woolwich.
Perhaps the choice was not very wise, for the bleak
air tried her, and it was impossible to leave the house
without a steep walk up or down hill. Before the
winter it became necessary to remove her to a warmer
climate, and Torquay was the place selected. At first
'the delight of getting down again to Devonshire,
which was her native county,' seemed to revive her;
and Mr. Jukes was able to preach at Torquay and at
Babbicombe, and once or twice to go to London. But
her 'delight in seeing the red cliffs and wooded hills'
could not restore her wasted strength.

Rest came in May 1880. She was carried to
Hull for burial; and Mr. Jukes returned to his soli-
tary house at Woolwich, where his patience and faith
soon enabled him to resume literary work, and to
complete what seems to some of his readers the most
perfect of all his books. During the months of
anxiety he had endeavoured to write out the substance of a course of lectures on the passages in St.
John's Gospel in which the phrase, 'Verily, verily,'

occurs, and which he regarded as describing various successive stages of the growth of the New Man in us. The book was published in 1881 under the title of 'The New. Man, and the Eternal Life.' This was followed in 1888 by 'The Names of God in Holy Scripture,' in which the various Names given to God in Genesis were regarded as displaying various revelations of Him. At this time, though his health was somewhat infirm, he was able to attend many meetings in London, especially those of a society called 'Clerical Friends in Council,' which had been founded by the Rev. G. H. Wilkinson and others, and consisted of clergymen of very various schools, who met monthly to discuss theological questions. At these meetings he was always an honoured speaker. He was also engaged in an enormous correspondence; for his works were widely read in England and America, and had been translated into several languages; and many of his readers wrote to him of their difficulties or, perhaps, their crotchets. His last literary work was a little volume on 'The Order and Connexion of the Church's Teaching, as set forth in the Arrangement of the Epistles and Gospels.' This was published in 1893.

As old age advanced, it brought with it rheumatism and some affection of the heart, so that moving

c

and writing were alike difficult. In other respects he
was in fair health ; he enjoyed visits from his friends,
and at times was able to converse with them with
little diminution of his mental power. He was
always bright and thankful : the words, 'Thank God,
all things are for us, and not against us,' were constantly on his lips. To one who loved him, and
whom he had been the first to bless after her marriage in 1874, he continued his tone of affectionate
teasing till she saw him last in 1896. As weakness
increased, he was induced to give up his house at
Woolwich, and to make his home with his elder son
at Hackney. In the autumn of 1900 he went to visit
his daughter at Southampton, from whose words is
transcribed this account of his closing days :

In March (1901) he had a slight attack of faintness.
It only lasted a few moments, but alarmed his maid very
much. I was not present. When I saw him about ten
minutes afterwards he said he was all right, but he looked
strange. In a few days, however, he was as active as usual
again, taking his walk daily in the little park near the
house, or on the western shore, which he much enjoyed
when the tide was up. He went there nearly every day.
On May 1 he brought me two baskets of strawberries
for my birthday, and was distressed that he had forgotten
it until the evening. This was the last time he walked
so far. Ten days afterwards he was again very poorly,
and I noticed a distinct change in him. The intense rest-

lessness increased ; and this was a marked feature throughout his illness. He was never quiet, and even when taking
a drive it seemed impossible to get him comfortable. . . .
He generally fell asleep from sheer exhaustion after so
much tossing ; and then he wandered very much.

On Wednesday, May 22, he told me he knew he was very
ill. . . . On this day he spoke to me much of my mother.
His thoughts seemed much with her, as indeed they ever
were. . . . On the 26th (Whitsunday) he remained in bed,
and only once got up again for a few hours. The first few
weeks in bed his mind was quite clear, and he enjoyed
being read to, and asked every day if there were any letters.
The last one I read to him was from Mr. Edward Clifford.
He especially enjoyed hymns being read or repeated to him,
and they seemed to quiet and soothe him more than anything else. . . . He was very peaceful and restful in spirit,
though the poor body was in such discomfort. He did
not, after the early days of his illness, allude to his departure, though he was quite aware it was drawing near. . . .
One evening, after a day of unusual distress, I said to him,
' You have had a very trying day.' He said, so sweetly,
'Oh, I could not say that. We must have trials here.
Through the Lord's mercy, I have no pain ; but I am
weary, weary, weary.'

The last week or ten days his mind seemed more
cloudy . . . he gradually fell into a comatose state, and
passed away peacefully, but quite unconscious, at 9.50 P.M.
July 4. His body was laid at Hull, by the side of that of
his wife.

LETTERS OF ANDREW JUKES

1851

THE ROMAN CHURCH

(To the Rev. F. W. Faber)

4 ,

IT was very pleasant to hear again, and to find that the old link of Harrow days still binds us so closely. Little did we think then how we might both some day be strangers to our brethren, or how far we might be carried apart even from each other, before we reached home. Outwardly you and I seem far enough apart; yet I find that many of those considerations which have, I may say, forced me into my present position. of loneliness and outward isolation were also those which unsettled you from that home of our spirits, where we had been born and nursed together. That Act of Uniformity, . . . together with the declaration of the Queen's (which, I suppose, means the Parliament's) supremacy in things spiritual as well as temporal, which has

B

already swept away I know not how many bishoprics
in Ireland, and may alter and sweep away everything we care for in the Church of England, has,
I find, been to you what it was to me, the barrier
which positively stopped my way, and forced me to
find some other path. But I have not been able so
quickly as you to find another home. I am yet in
spirit one of those who wander about in sheepskins
and goatskins, in deserts and in mountains, and in
dens and caves of the earth. Foxes have holes, but
I have found no home on earth. There are indeed
places where I can work, but none on earth where
I can rest.

You speak, however, as if you had now found rest
in the bosom of that which you call your true mother.
But is the Church of Rome indeed your mother?
Did she really bear you?   Was it at her breasts that
you were nursed?   Is she indeed the 'mother of us
all'? 'Jerusalem *which is above* is the mother of
us all,' who nurses us even while we are in the flesh,
but who is little known till heaven really opens to us.
And indeed, if the Church could be seen, why put it
into the Creed?   Why say, 'I believe in the Holy
Catholic Church'? For faith, surely, is the substance
of things hoped for and unseen.   If we see this Holy
Catholic Church, why put it into the Creed among

the unseen verities which faith alone can deal with?
Not that I deny to the Roman Church a large share
of precious truth. To my mind she seems to have
perhaps more truth than any other local Church.
She puts more bread upon her table, a richer, broader
fare; but, unless I greatly err, all her loaves with
the precious wheat of truth have the poison of awful
lies mingled. And this poison seems to me in too
many cases to outweigh the truth, and make it
inoperative. The Catholic element is there, and this
is truth. But the Roman is there also, the lust for
boundless rule, which brings all into bondage, and
this is false. So, at least, when seeking to weigh all
this in the presence of God, it has appeared to me.
Had it not been so, I should long ere this have
followed you. But I could not be true to what I see
of truth—I could not walk with God even according
to my poor measure—and yet submit my conscience
to Rome. Great as are to me the difficulties of the
Church of England, I should find tenfold more in
Rome. With others brought up by her I doubt not
it may be different. God will judge them by what
they have, not by what they have not. They have
never known, as by grace I have, an open Bible,
which, while of course it needs an interpreter, is yet
'able to make us wise unto salvation through faith

which is in Christ Jesus.' By this I have been
formed, by this I have been led, to try to walk with
Christ, to deal with Him, to hear His voice, to have
Him speaking to me, to let His eyes of fire search me
through and through in all things. . . .

But I must conclude. I did not think of saying
all this. I wished rather to thank you for your loving
words, and for the promise of your prayers. Prayers
always help us, if they are prayers of love and faith.
Meanwhile, and ever, the Lord cares for both of us;
for is He not the Good Shepherd? And in all our
wanderings, and in our captivities, wherever for our
own or the Church's sins we may be driven in these
last difficult days, He can and will not only be a
sanctuary to us, if we love Him, but will, I trust,
overrule even our wanderings, so as to make them
just that discipline which we each may need.

1862

THE FALL

Consider whether nature and life, as it now is, is
really normal—whether the condition of things as
they now are is not a fall, out of which God is surely
delivering us, but which nevertheless is a fall, and

no more normal than hell is normal. Not to speak
of any hell but what we see, you will, I am sure,
allow that most souls are restless and unsatisfied,
and that thousands are deluded, mad, miserable,
helpless. This is simple fact. Now, is this normal?
Is this misery, madness, hopelessness, and restlessness, God's creature, or is it a fall? Is it the proper
progress of souls whose origin is from God? Is it
the normal course of training His sons and creatures,
or is it the result (surely overruled by His almighty
power and wisdom for good) of a fall from Him?

An old book, which some people think helps to
solve the riddle, says this present state is not normal,
but a fall. To me it seems that nature and man
declare the same. Man, even by nature, is ashamed
of being what he is, both as to body and spirit. The
natural functions of his body are a shame to him. . . .
And, as to his spirit, the natural tendency of it is
ever to manifest shame at being what he is—witness
the thoughts of the heart in all, and the attempt of
all to hide from others what they are, and to appear
different from what they really are ; as, for instance,
a coward to appear brave, and a fool a wise man.

Now, a dunghill within each of us, and a poor
restless vain heart, may seem to you normal enough
for the love of God, though we are all even naturally

ashamed of it.   And leprosy, palsy, blindness, deaf-
ness, fever, madness, and all the rest of the miseries
which Christ cures in the Gospel, may seem to you
a due 'order.'   To me they are all disorder.   And,
because they are such, Christ heals them ; humanity
in its present order, or disorder, not being able to
meet the evil. . . .

Because I hold this state to be a fall, you charge
me with ' deplorable hopelessness,' and with saying
that ' God has abandoned the world.'   Why, I abhor
the very idea of God abandoning us.   My faith is,
that, in spite of the awful fall of spirits, be we where
we may in our fall, in nature or in hell, God comes
where we are for us, coming into the creature's fall
to be its life again.   This is the old Gospel.   But
this is very different from holding what I understand
you to say, that the fallen state is normal and in due
' order.'

As to what you say of our extraordinary insensi-
bility to the peril of those we love, and the death
which is around on every hand, it is indeed a great
mystery.   But you might put your question much
more broadly—not only, ' How can we eat and drink
with the possibility of a future death for any near
and dear to us ? ' but how we eat and drink with a
present death around us, constantly smiting those
nearest and dearest to us ; how we can be easy while

thousands of creatures, as innocent as we are, are in suffering and have to die to support us daily. It is a great mystery. I do not know why they perish. I do not know anything about their future. Their life is a mystery to me. So is that of beast-like, brutish men. Nor do I know why there are so many untimely births of children, perhaps as many as those which see the light.

The other point between us is the Bible. May I ask you to weigh one question? Is the book of nature a revelation of God? You say, 'Yes;' and I also say yes, though with reservation. For nature is to me a revelation of God, but only of God working in a certain sphere, and that a fallen one. Well, then, nature being God's book, and a revelation of Him, as you assent, how does nature reveal Him? Be honest. Look at death reigning in nature, and say, 'Is the revelation nature gives of God better than that the Bible gives of Him? Are not exactly the same contradictions and the same difficulties in both the revelations?' Either, then, you must say, 'Nature is a lying book, and therefore I will not believe the facts of geology, of death and judgment of whole races of creatures formed by my Father;' or you must confess that there is some riddle both in nature and the Bible as revelations of God, as yet too deep for you.

1865

TRIALS THE WAY TO GOD'S KINGDOM

As to your inward trial and perplexity, is it not the universal experience, sooner or later, of all God's true children ? . . . Still, you may ask, granting that such trial is not uncommon, why is it permitted ? Is it not a mark of our unfaithfulness ? I answer by asking another question. Are thorns in the flesh and messengers of Satan marks of our unfaithfulness ? Is it God's way to take them away when we pray, or does He not rather teach us under them, and even by them, that His grace is sufficient for us ? For how does God's kingdom come in us ? Is it by the removal of all outward and inward impediments to our spirit ? Is it by taking away all hindrances to our wisdom, righteousness, or freedom ? This would be *my* kingdom. This would result in self being exalted and strong, even if we were not conscious of it. How many have proved this, who, to get God's kingdom, as they thought, have disengaged themselves from all outward things, and have found at last that it is ' my kingdom,' poor self after all, instead of ' Thy kingdom.' For indeed it is by self-despair, the fruit of trial, and so of knowing our own weakness and wretchedness, that we come to God's kingdom. The Church will have to prove this, just as every individual must. It will not be her efforts, or her successes, or her rule, or her exaltation, that will bring in the real kingdom of God in the world. Such successes will always end, as we see in Popery, in being substantially '*my* kingdom,' not '*Thy* kingdom.' But our prayer is, 'Thy kingdom come.' And whenever this comes, either in us or in the earth, it comes by the breaking up of all that man can boast in. God will bring it in, as He pleases. We cannot do it, either by our solitude or by our preachings. When we have really learned this, the kingdom we sigh for is not far off. The truth is, we are such poor creatures, so easily puffed up, so soon conceited, that God can only save us by breaking us in pieces. And our goodness and religiousness needs to be broken to pieces as much as our badness; for self can get into religion, and cleave more closely to it, and hide more subtly in it, than in ungodliness. So in one way or another self is pursued to the death. 'Thou turnest man to destruction.' But all this is but the way to build up a better life. 'Again Thou sayest, Come again, ye children of men.' Come again, thou little child, who shalt be able unhurt to put thy hand on the cockatrice's den.

1866

SPIRITISM

I have not a doubt that the departed are often very near us, and that it is possible (I do not say that it is right, or even desirable) for us to have communion with them. God, for wise and loving reasons, when man fell into selfhood, shut him out from Paradise or the spirit-world, because, being what he then was, a selfish creature, the laws of the spirit-world, by which like inevitably gravitates to like, would necessarily bring fallen man into contact not with the best but [the] worst part of the spirit-world. But, though man in selfhood, the Old Adam as the Scripture calls it, is lovingly shut out from Paradise or the spirit-world, the New Man is called to enter there, when he is fit for it, as we see in Christ, who, as Son of man, whilst He was upon the earth, at times, as at the Transfiguration, had converse with departed souls, for He then spoke with Moses and Elias. We see the same thing in St. John (Rev. xxii. 8, 9), and also in St. Paul (2 Cor. xii. 2–4). The same is also true of all the prophets, who were clairvoyants. But whilst this access into the spirit-world is safe to unselfish and meek and loving souls,

who are partakers of the Divine life through Jesus
Christ, it is most dangerous to ordinary men, for the
reason I have already given you, namely, that in the
spirit-world like always meets with like; and therefore
[it] is absolutely forbidden to natural men, as we see
both in the Old Testament and in the New.   (See
Deut. xviii. 9–15, and Galatians v. 20.)   Witchcraft
or necromancy, that is, the power to deal with the
departed, is a faculty of our nature, for man was made
for the spirit-world; and yet to use it naturally, that
is, in selfhood and self-will, is most perilous.   In a
word, there are two ways into the spirit-world—one
by magic arts in self-will, when the thing is most
dangerous; the other, by communion with Christ
and His Cross, when the spirit-world opens of itself
to God's saints, when it is safe; though even in
this latter case, as we see in Peter at the Transfiguration, there is a temptation to make tabernacles
for Moses and Elias, that is, to worship the departed :
as we see in the Church of Rome, which is Peter's
Church.

MARRIAGE

Marriage may be one of the greatest of your
spiritual blessings if it is, as it ought to be, the
constant witness of Christ's love to us—how He

ends all separation—how He finds His joy in the creature which He has called to share His name.

1868

THE WAY OF THE CROSS

If the dear souls who say every week, ' By Thy Baptism, Fasting, and Temptation ; by Thine Agony and bloody Sweat; by Thy Cross and Passion, Good Lord, deliver us,' only knew the meaning of the words they utter, how it would astonish them. They have not thought that in this prayer they are asking to be brought out of nature on the same highway of the holy Cross by which our Head went forth; for while we are in nature we are in wrath—' By nature children of wrath.'

REGENERATION

Regeneration, as St. Paul describes it, and as I feel it, is not a mere covering of the old man with any imputed righteousness, but it is a true bringing forth of a new life and a new man, which is Christ in us, the hope of glory. New clothes put upon an old man do not make a new man ; and yet with some this is all the idea they have, and this is all that Evangelicalism teaches as to our 'being made the righteousness of God in Christ.' But the incorruptible Seed of the Word does not lie dead, but quickens a new man, which needs and has its proper meat and drink in the flesh and blood of the Son of man. I believe, yea, I know, that the holy blood of Jesus Christ is as necessary to form a spiritual, immortal, incorruptible body, garment, or house, for God to dwell in, as the blood of the woman under death is necessary to produce this present outward body of corruption, weakness, and misery. We become by faith in Christ as truly bone of His bone and flesh of His flesh (which surely is not the flesh of this tabernacle in which we groan being burdened), as we are bone and flesh, that is, of the substance, of our earthly parents.

1869

KNOWLEDGE AND WISDOM. MALE AND FEMALE

I am conscious that one characteristic of my mind, which, if it has sometimes through God's mercy helped me, has also more than once, especially in my earlier days, hindered me from learning, has been the liking I have to see things definitely, and the innate dislike I have always had to indefiniteness and indistinctness; and to this day the same natural tendency clings to me; though it is years and years since I saw that what is *definite* cannot, from the very nature of things, comprehend or express the infinite, and that all definitions, just because they are definitions, must limit and narrow any deep spiritual truth in its fullness. *Defining* seems to me to have been one of the curses of Protestantism, and one of the necessary results of its intellectual character. Definitions can indeed map out the surface for us, and they are useful for this, if we remember that it is the surface. . . . We go on from the 'word of knowledge,' which deals with the surface of things, or things as they appear, to the 'word of wisdom,' or things as they really are. . . .

I see . . . how not only the Church is male and female in different aspects, sometimes symbolised by the Woman in heaven or by the Mother of our Lord, sometimes by our Lord Himself and His body; but also how our very Lord Himself is also Head, or masculine, to us, while God is Head or Bridegroom to Him. My question is, or was meant to be, Which is the *perfecter state*—to be as a Christed soul, embracing (to use Behmen's common expression) the Virgin Sophia; or that the soul as a bride, that is, passive and feminine, should be embraced by the heavenly Bride-

groom ?   I suppose some souls here develop more of
the masculine or intellectual, some more of the feminine or passive and affectional form, in their progress
towards the glorious end.   But the language at the
end of the Bible seems to me to say that the end of ends
will see the creature feminine, and God all in all.

1870

SALVATION BY GRACE

Fancy a man only kept from stealing by fearing
to be sent to gaol.   What sort of honesty would this
be ?   St. Paul says, ' The grace of God which brings
salvation, teaches us to deny ungodliness ; ' and
again, that ' hope brings forth fruit in us, since we
knew the grace of God in truth.'

1871

SUBSTITUTION

As to the question of *substitution*, while, as you
know, I entirely dissent from the popular pseudo-
Evangelical doctrine, that Christ took our place that
we should not take it, and died that *we should not
die*, and suffered that *we should not suffer*—all of

which is not only opposed to Scripture, but to fact and experience—I yet hold that Christ did stand in our place and under our burden, which is the exact sense of the word *substitute*. . . . If Christ did not stand in our place and under our burden, and so take upon Himself our weaknesses, our death, and our curse, why did He die? Why was He accursed? I answer, He was accursed because He stood in our place, in our nature, under our burden, for us. He did not stand under it that we should not stand under it, which is what the pseudo-Evangelical school teaches; but He stood under it because we were under it: by standing under it to make us one with Himself, and so lift us in and with and by Himself, by the resurrection of the dead, out of our lot into His lot. He stood under our burden. He stood under it for us. This is *substitution*. If you deny this true sense of the word, taught in Scripture and all the early Fathers, you give the pseudo-Evangelicals a strong handle against you. . . . But this is only half the truth. He also stands in our place and under our burdens by uniting Himself to each of us *now*, so that it is not only we which live, but Christ liveth in us. . . . Just as when He took flesh of the Virgin, and stood for us in our lot, He lifted the nature, into the place of which and under the burden of which He had come, by His resurrection up to God's right hand : so now, by coming to dwell in us, He stands yet under our burden, and bears it for us, bidding us cast all our burdens and cares upon the Lord, that so He may lift us with Him by a resurrection from the dead in due time to God's right hand. . . . But, because some muddle-headed people, calling themselves Evangelicals, put a wrong and absurd sense on the word *substitution*, you deny the true sense of the word, which yet is the only ground on which you can hope for deliverance from the curse, and the only explanation of Christ's becoming a curse at all. As to your friend, the Independent minister, not objecting to your view of substitution, I am not surprised at all. The Dissenting bodies as a rule have all been brought up in the pseudo-Evangelical doctrine, that Christ died that we should not die, and suffered that we should not suffer. When they see the falsity of this, if they have not the Catholic faith to fall back on, there is every probability of their going to the opposite extreme, and denying that Christ took our place or standing for us ; in other words, that He was a substitute. But truth is not to be given up because it is caricatured.

PRIESTHOOD

Your questions as to priesthood are weighty, and timely too; for the days are come for Israel to go out for ever from the house of bondage; and as a sign of this, the first-born of Egypt (the first-born are the priests and kings), of that Egypt where our Lord is crucified, are everywhere being smitten. Is not kingship and priesthood smitten everywhere throughout Europe?

I certainly do not object to the statement . . . that a special priesthood of some for others remains in the Christian, even as it certainly existed throughout the Jewish dispensation. You say you now doubt this. . . . You are now disposed to think that this special priesthood was peculiar to Judaism, and has no place whatever in the Christian Church. I do not think so. I think the allusion in St. Jude's Epistle to the sin of Korah as a thing not only possible but actually committed in the Christian Church shows that some in the Church must be priests in a special way; for Korah's sin was his saying to Moses and Aaron, 'Ye take too much upon you, seeing all the congregation is holy, every one of them.' Do you not see, too, that if Israel's history is, as you confess, the type of ours, there must be some meaning in all that is laid down so distinctly respecting the old priesthood? Nor does the verse you quote from 1 Pet. ii. as to all Christians being a 'royal priesthood' disprove that some among them may more specially be called to priestly service; for the words you cite are a quotation from Ex. xix. and were originally used of the whole Old Testament Israel; and yet some of them, as you allow, had a special priesthood. . . .

The key to the question lies, I believe, in the distinction between *our calling* and *our attainment*. In Christ all are called to be priests; yet only some have apprehended what they are apprehended for. What is priestly work but standing before God and offering for others? Do you really think all Christians offer for others? Do you think that the words in St. John xx. as to loosing and binding are said to all Christians, or even to all converted souls? You confess that they speak of special privileges; but are not the special privileges referred to distinctly priestly? I think they are. I think, therefore, that there is a special priesthood of some more than others in the Christian Church, some only entering into or apprehending that which all are called to in Christ Jesus. What the priesthood is to which these are called—whether it is carnal or spiritual—received

by a knowledge of Christ in the flesh or in the Spirit,
is another and quite distinct, but most important,
subject.

I go on now to your second question. And here
I quite agree with you that the outward and suc-
cessional priesthood of the fleshly Church, though it
has its place and was ordained by Christ Himself, is
not, as you have experimentally discovered, the true
Melchisedek-priesthood of the New Covenant. . . . It is
hard to speak on this or any other spiritual point
without being misapprehended, for in speaking of the
higher and spiritual knowledge of Christ, which you
aspire to, I shrink from seeming to say a word against
that lower and fleshly knowledge of Him, which in
many of God's truest children precedes the higher
knowledge. Yet the fact remains, that there are these
two knowledges of Him. We may know Him after
the flesh or in the Spirit; both of which are spoken
of by St. Paul, when he says, ' Henceforth know we
no man after the flesh. Yea, though we have known
Christ after the flesh, yet now henceforth know we
Him no more ; ' and again, when, after he had
suffered the loss of all things for Christ, he prays to
' know Him, and the power of His resurrection, and
the fellowship of His sufferings.' The former knowledge of Christ, that after the flesh, is figured in the

relation of the disciples to Christ as shown throughout the Four Gospels, when they knew Christ as
separate from and outside of them : the latter,
in their relation to Him after they knew His
resurrection and the promised coming of the Holy
Ghost. In the one, we see our experience when, like
the disciples, though we may have left all to follow
Him, and have been ordained and sent out to preach
the Gospel by Him, yea, and to know that the devils
are subject to us through His Name, we yet are carnal,
as we prove when the Cross meets us with all its
shame and bitterness. In the other, we see that later
experience, only known when we have gone through
the trial of losing Him after the flesh, and have come
through an experimental knowledge of His Cross to
that promised baptism of the Spirit which is our
Pentecost, when tongues of fire are given us, and a
mighty rushing wind works with us in our ministry.
Of these, the first is connected with our knowledge of
Christ in fleshly forms ; that is, our knowledge of Him
in His outward Church, His sacraments, His ministry,
His written Word—all of which are, as has been most
truly said, 'extensions of the Incarnation '—all which,
like the knowledge of Christ in the flesh by His disciples of old, has to give place, if we go onward, to
another deeper knowledge of Him, no longer as out-

side of and separate from us, but as living His own life and doing His own works in and by us; which last is only reached, now as of old, by an experience answering to that of the disciples, who, when they are brought by the Cross to lose Him in one form that they may know Him in another, seem to think that their hope has failed, for they say, 'We thought that it had been He who would have redeemed Israel;' though at this very point, and by this very experience of utter self-despair, they are being introduced to the deeper and higher knowledge of the same Jesus.

This, I know, is the appointed path. I myself have trod it. And it is through this experience that we are brought from the carnal or fleshly laying on of Christ's hands, which we receive of Him through His fleshly members, when we only know Him after the flesh, to another very different ordination, also from Him, when 'the hand of the Lord is upon us' (Ezek. i. 3), when our Pentecost comes, and we receive the promised power, answering to that which Christ shed forth of old at Pentecost, in virtue of which we are like Him made priests after the order of Melchisedek.

Christ's own life figures both stages. He is the pattern of His elect; and just as He, having been begotten of the Holy Ghost, and as such being from that very hour the Son of God and the Holy One of God, was yet for a while bound in Jewish swaddling-clothes, and then, as in the flesh, grew in wisdom and stature, and asked questions of the doctors at Jerusalem, all of which was in some sense carnal and Jewish, until in Jordan He came to quite another experience, when heaven opened to Him and the Spirit descended on Him, which was His Pentecost; after which went He forth in true priestly work, as dead and risen through that mystic baptism; so is it with His members; for we, though sons of God from the day when by the Word the New Man is formed in us, may yet, and must yet, be bound with Jewish swaddling-clothes, and in the flesh, and occupied with Jewish ordinances and passovers for a season, before heaven opens to us. But if we go on we shall surely reach the stage when, through an inward and mystic death, heaven opens to us, and the Spirit like a dove comes down, and the voice of the Father is heard, saying, 'Thou art My beloved child.' This is something very different from our first quickening in Christ; as different as Christ's experience after heaven opened to Him was from that which He had had to that hour. And it is after we have reached this stage that we are priests indeed, though called to the self-same priesthood from the first. In a word, 'As

Christ is, so are we.' Even of Him it could be said,
' If He were on earth, He should not be a priest;'
for His true priesthood is not the earthly priesthood.
So it is only as we grow up in Him, as dead and
risen with Him, and so brought from the natural and
carnal to the spiritual, that we reach that priesthood
which, I thank God, you are now longing to enter on.

If you understand this, you will see what I mean
when I say that all Christians do not at once know
this priesthood. The Corinthians, though Christians,
did not know it, for they were ' carnal.' They therefore needed the priestly service of one like Paul both to
bind and loose them in many matters. Nay, even
Christ did not know it as in the flesh. He did not know
it till, by a mystic but very real death, heaven, as He
came up out of Jordan, opened to Him. He was only
a priest in resurrection. We too, like Him, are only
priests as we ' know the power of His resurrection.'

SACRAMENTS

I would ask you to consider, if baptism is not the
sacrament of our regeneration, what is it? You
know how the New Testament speaks of baptism.
Say that the statements refer to the baptism of
believers, yet even then they are very remarkable;
for who in baptising even adults, and with the

greatest care as to the admission of proper candidates,
can say that all have true faith? and yet St. Paul
says to the carnal Galatian Church, of which he stood
in doubt, fearing almost that his labour among or
for them had been in vain, ' As many of you as have
been baptised into Christ have put on Christ.' And
so as to the Supper of the Lord. It was to the
Corinthians, to whom he could not write as unto
spiritual but as to carnal, that he says, ' He that
eateth and drinketh unworthily eateth and drinketh
damnation to himself, not discerning the Lord's
body.' And again, ' Wherefore, whosoever eats of this
bread or drinks of this cup unworthily shall be guilty
of the body and blood of the Lord.'. . . Surely, if Peter
is right, there is a blessed sense in which our nature,
condemned in Him by His cross, is yet ' begotten
again by His resurrection;' and surely baptism, if it
is anything, is just this profession of our faith, that,
dead as we are by nature (and thus we are ' buried in
baptism,' for we do not bury live things but dead
things), we are also quickened again in Christ by His
resurrection. Is not the sacrament a pledge and
witness of what Christ is for us? We do indeed
confess in it what we are—we are dead; but we also
confess what Christ is—that all our hope is in Him,
and that He, having taken our place, the place of all,

is now for all at God's right hand. On this ground,
and on this alone, can we go and baptise all nations.

I wish time and my limits would permit me to go
into all that gathers round this question. To do it
properly we should have to look at the truth which
underlies what is called the 'Sacramental System.'
For there is a great truth underlying that system;
for the whole Gospel system, as a dispensation to
men, is sacramental.   Christ Himself, the Divine
Word linked with and manifested in union with a
creature, is the greatest of all sacraments, and
the ground and reason of all of them. He is 'an outward and visible sign of an inward and spiritual grace
given to us.' He is 'a means whereby we receive the
same, and a pledge to assure us thereof.' He is not
only 'a pledge to assure us thereof,' which is all the
so-called Evangelical party will allow to sacraments,
but He is also 'a means whereby we receive the same.'
To open all this would require one to go into the needs-
be and reason for the Holy Incarnation. Why did
God's Son come in the flesh ? Why did the Word of
God reveal Himself in human and creature form ?
The answer is found in man's state, and in God's love,
which stooped to meet man where he was and as he
could bear it ; because being fallen he could not see
God as He is, but could only apprehend and receive

Him when He took some form which man could receive even while he was yet in darkness. Therefore the Divine Word all through the former dispensation came under carnal veils and forms ; I mean, the Jewish ordinances ; for only so could a carnal people apprehend Him. Therefore, for the same reason, He came in the flesh of Christ, not only by Christ's death to witness to the need of the death of self if we would re-enter Paradise, and in Him and by His sacrifice to slay the enmity, but also that He might by the bands of a man, by human love and truth and human sympathies, draw some to Him, who, having first known Him only carnally, or in the flesh, might in due time know Him spiritually. Therefore He gave us a Bible, not all New Testament ; and therefore yet and always He speaks to man first by a letter or law, which is a form, before He speaks by His Spirit or in the Gospel. Therefore too He gave us baptism and the Supper of the Lord, forms like Himself, in which there is the union of the Word of God and a creature, that so by the creature-form, whether of water or of bread and wine, He might reach some who could not at first apprehend all that His Word is in itself, or even all that His Word in union with these creatures would say to them. Sacraments, therefore, in a very true and blessed sense, are, as

some have said, not witnesses only but even extensions
of the Incarnation, because in them the Word by a
creature-form reaches some souls—because in them
the Word yet comes 'in the flesh.' The Word surely
comes to us ' in the flesh ' when it comes out of the
heart of some loving soul who preaches the Gospel;
for the Word, in coming out of such a heart, takes
the form of that heart, and comes in human guise, not
as it would appear to angels or seraphs in heaven, but
as it has appeared to him who proclaims it, and as it
can appear to men. So too does this Word come likewise in sacraments, by an acted rather than by a
spoken word—though there is ever also a spoken word
in a sacrament—yet ever with a word speaking to men,
if they can hear, and saying more to one and less to
another, exactly according to their capacity. Thus
sacraments are, and must be, to men infinitely different
to different receivers; for some, the carnal, see only the
outward form; and some, just as they become spiritual,
see the Spirit which is speaking under it. With many,
however, the objection to the sacramental system is
really the objection to the Incarnation. Men see
the form, and do not believe that the Word of God is
with it, or the power of that Word, even in that
humble form, if men will but trust it. Like the Jews of
old, they say practically, ' This is only the carpenter's

Son : His father and mother we know.' ' This is only water, or this is only bread ; ' not seeing that the Divine Word may be there with the outward form, able to give through it, or out of it, or at least by it, unfathomed draughts of God's fullness.

1872

THE RESURRECTION BODY

To me for years it has been gradually appearing (contrary to all my received opinions, ' received by tradition from my fathers '), first, that the resurrection body is a gradual growth, formed (analogously to the natural body) on the germ of the spiritual and resurrection life, quickened at conversion by the Divine Seed, that is, the Word ; which body, when it has reached a certain stage of growth, comes forth from the womb of present nature, this coming forth being what is called the resurrection ; and that, therefore, the resurrection body is not (as so many say) an instantaneous creation put from without upon an unclothed spirit, which for years or ages has been unclothed in Hades, but rather, like all God's other works, a gradually formed and perfected work ; and secondly, that for this reason their resurrection body is reached or gained at different times by different members of Christ, the Head coming forth first, and the other members just as they grow up into Him, each according to their fitness for this great change.

MALE AND FEMALE

As to the enigma with which you conclude (as to our being ' divided duals '), I may say that I have long been face to face with the riddle, but do not yet see the full answer to it. I see how, by Incarnation, Christ came into our divided humanity, that He was a man and not a woman, and consequently was circumcised upon the eighth day. I see, too, that as seen by John in resurrection, He has ' paps,' that is to say, woman's breasts. . . . Further, I see that the first form of the New Man when it is formed in us by the Divine Word is, like Christ when born of Mary, in the divided humanity, that is, a man or a male (cf. υἱὸν ἄρσεν, Rev. xii. 5, an apparent tautology, but with meaning), and not, as it becomes through the Cross, that new creature, ' where there is neither male nor female,' but where the two are made one in Christ. But what the two are I cannot describe, or how the man becomes the woman and the woman the man, or rather how each becomes both, I cannot say,

save that it is through death. Certainly, I do not
look for a fleshly helpmeet to a spiritual man ; nor,
as it appears to me, is ‘ some perfected female saint ’
the God-appointed helpmeet of the New Man. I do
not say that we may not have to go through a divided
stage even beyond bodily death, but I look for an end
of all division. Here, however, at present I only see
Noah’s hill-tops. I see that, at first, as men we
embrace truths as women—witness all the typical
men, Abraham, Isaac, and Jacob, all whose wives,
according to Paul, . . . are certain truths or principles—as Hagar, law, and Sarah, gospel. But I see
that at last, when the marriage of the Lamb is come,
He, the Truth, is Husband, and we are brides. . . .
One consideration which may contain the clue to
much of this is the fact that we, or any other
creature, may at the same time, even when still in
the divided form, be either male or female, according
as it is regarded in relation to what is below or what
is above it. The man is head of the woman—he is
male to her ; but while this is so, he is feminine to
Christ, who is his Head. So, again, Christ, who is
Head of the body, or male to me, while male or husband to us is feminine to God, who is His Head,
according to 1 Cor. xi. 3. I see the same thing in
Nature. Water is male to earth, quickening and

making it fruitful. But water . . . is feminine to air ; that is, air has power to come into and cover it and be its head. Just as air, again, itself is feminine to light and heat, which in like manner can come into it and head it.

TRUE SPIRITUALITY

The Lord Himself seems now to me to be the true pattern of spirituality; and His spirituality, if I understand it, was not in getting up as high as possible, so high that few could reach Him, but in coming down in the likeness of sinful men, into their form, into their place, into their curse, for them. I can imagine no higher spirituality for man than that seen in the Incarnation ; for that Incarnation was self-sacrifice, and self-sacrifice seems to me now to be the essence and test of true spirituality. Therefore, even when in our likeness and upon earth, in our place and bearing our infirmities, He could truly say, ' He that hath seen Me hath seen the Father ; ' for God is love ; and herein was love, to come down into the place and form of sinners. And Jesus Christ, who once came in the flesh, inasmuch as He is ever the same, to this day comes in the flesh and in fleshly forms, which some who lack His spirit of self-sacrificing love think unspiritual.

SEPARATION

If the state of the Church offends you—and, alas ! it is too plain that the Church is fallen—would it not have been well if you could have sought some retreat for a while, where, like John or Paul, or the Lord Himself in the wilderness, you might in secret and silence, out of the stir of controversy, have asked not what is wrong, for this is pretty plain, but what is the right path with regard to it ? It is easy to see what is amiss : it is difficult to know what to do to serve a fallen Church. You say, however, that you are ' now happily out of the world-church, and pastor of the Free Church.' As to the ' world-church,' I do not justify it. Let us assume that it is the woman taken in adultery, in the very act. But the question remains, What are we to do ? Are we to stone her ? The Master says, ' Let him that is without sin cast the first stone.' If the so-called Free Church is ' without sin '—if the various dissenting bodies are ' without sin '—let them stone away. Can you read the miserable extract you send me from the S. paper, and think that the writer, who flings stones so cleverly, is ' without sin ' ? And as to your ' Free Church,' is it a Church at all ? And if a Church, what is it ' free ' from ? What is a Church ? Where

D

does it differ from a company, a society, an alliance?
Is the Evangelical Alliance a Church? And what,
I would ask again, is the so-called Free Church free
from? You say the National Church is hampered
by the State, and cannot put away the evil which is
in it. Granted. What then? Can you put away
all the evil which is within you? Are you, therefore,
to go out of yourself and commit suicide? Can you
really think that you will not be hampered where
you are by persons holding a certain relationship to
your ' Free Church,' who will do all sorts of things?
Or do you think that you will be able to put away the
evil which must sooner or later appear among you?
What is the evil of evils but self-love and self-will?
See it rampant in every form of dissent—in almost
all Christians. How are you, in your ' Free Church,'
to put away this evil? Is not the real truth this,
that the Church is fallen, and, being fallen, is it not
a pretence to say that we can make a part of it ' free,'
while the rest is suffering? But the Lord will teach
you, and teach you as He has had to teach most of
us, by mistakes. The only way to help some dear
souls is to let them go wrong and fall. Thus only
are they delivered from their natural haste and self-
confidence. Thanks be to God, He can, and does,
overrule what He does not directly rule. He will,

I trust, do so in your case. I am, however, astonished
at the reason you give for joining the 'Free Church.'
It is because Mr. Bennett and others like him are
permitted in the Church of England. You could
allow men like the Essayists and Reviewers, who
denied the Atonement and Inspiration and nearly
everything else supernatural, to remain in the
Church. Their being there did not drive you out.
But Mr. Bennett's being allowed forces you to secede.
You will some day see clearer the difference between
the *cause* and the *occasion*.

1873

OBJECTORS TO RESTITUTION

When I think of my own life, though from my
first conversion through grace I have only desired
to give myself and all that I had for Christ; when I
see how for years, just like a child, accepting much
while others lacked, I could receive without a question
to be, like Jacob, loved, while others, like Esau, were,
I believed, for ever cast out; when, like Israel, I could
without compunction be joyous at my freedom from
Egypt, without a thought of the sacrifice of Egypt's
first-born, or of 'Ethiopia and Seba given for me;'

content if I found grace, though others by hundreds perished all around : when I remember all this, and how slowly my eyes opened to see why any are elect, even that ' if the firstfruit be holy, the lump should be holy also,' I cannot judge others who are satisfied with their own salvation, and are slow to learn why they are saved. If, therefore, there is any truth such brethren cannot yet receive, or if they judge me because I see in Scripture what they as yet do not, I do not press either myself or the truth God gives me upon them, because I know there is another present Teacher, and that when these brethren feel their need of further teaching and seek it, what they need will not be withheld.

GOD'S TWO METHODS

God is the only Teacher who has had, and yet has, two distinct methods, to meet two different stages of His children : namely, first law, then Gospel ; first letter, then spirit ; first nature, then grace ; first an outward, then an inward, witness. At the earlier stages what is spiritual is above us. . . . At such a stage souls need authority for truth. They cannot yet take truth for authority.

THE TEST OF A GOOD BOOK

The test I have found most useful to myself as to
the real use of any book is to mark the state of mind
in which I lay it down. If after reading it I am
humbler and nearer to God, in the sense of my
nothingness and His amazing love and wisdom, the
book is a good one, at least to me. If, on the other
hand, wonderful as the book may be, it leaves me, or
I leave it, thrown off from love (for God is love) into
all kinds of speculations, then the book to me, possibly through my own fault, has not been wholesome.

1874

REST

As to your question, growing out of the words or
feelings of your friend on the subject of the Christian's
immediate enjoyment of perfect rest, . . . probably
you mean one thing and she another when you speak
of 'rest.' For there are many 'rests' in the
Christian life. There is, first, the 'rest' which a
poor soul has while yet a captive in Egypt, resting
in safety under the sprinkled blood, though the
destroying angel is abroad. . . . This is a 'rest'
which we are all called to have as soon as we hear

and believe what is told us of the sprinkled Blood.
But even here there may be souls safe under the
sprinkled Blood who yet have fears, though, spite of
their fears, they are in perfect safety.   Then, again,
there is the 'rest' of the Sabbath, which God gives
to His people when they have got out into the wilderness.   This is the rest from our own works, to which
we are all called, but which souls yet bondsmen
in Egypt cannot know till they have crossed the Red
Sea. . . . Then, again (not to speak of the many
halts or resting-places by the way, some of which,
like Elim, are very pleasant, and all of which,
whether sweet or bitter, are providentially appointed
for us), there is in due time the 'rest' of Canaan for
us, that is, the rest we have when, passing over
Jordan, by a death to self, we can rest on some part
of the length and breadth of the rich ground of God's
promise, of which the land of promise was the figure.
Here we ought to be at rest, and the road here should
not be long.   Yet often it is long.   But even when
we reach this rest, it is not the perfect end.   Souls
may have reached this rest of Canaan who will yet
find that there is, as the apostle says, something
beyond it ; for, as he says, 'If Jesus (Joshua) had
given them rest, then would not David afterward have
spoken of another day.' . . . We may find, and must

find, that there is not only conflict in the land but also failure, as the Book of Judges shows so abundantly—failure from resting too soon, 'resting from war' (Josh. xi. 23), instead of going on to cut off the remnants of the adversaries. . . . Just as in these days many souls, having found peace to a certain extent, fail to go on to obtain all that is promised. . . . And whatever stage we may attain to here —even if we get on to know, as some have done, the glorious kingdom of the peaceful Son of David, when all seemed subdued, even then God's elect have to learn that there is a 'rest' yet further on; as it is said by the prophet even in Canaan, 'Arise and depart, for this is not your rest.' For Canaan is the type of the 'first heaven' or heavenly places; but the first heaven is 'shaken,' and is even seen by John to 'pass away,' before the perfect rest.

Of course faith can even now say of the last and highest of all these rests that it is already ours; for in this sense, if we believe, 'all things are ours, whether things present or things to come;' for 'faith is the substance of things hoped for, the conviction of things not seen.' But as a matter of experience comparatively few have reached the latter rests; for experience is the measure in which we have apprehended that which is ours already in Christ.

IMITATION OF CHRIST

How are we to walk so as to be conformed to Christ? Is it by setting this or that act or experience of His before us as the thing to be at once imitated? I should answer, where you are, there walk with God. Let every man abide in the calling wherein he is called. There live day by day by every word of God, eating Christ's flesh and drinking His blood; for the life can only grow by receiving its proper food. Covet, of course, the best things. But remember that the best thing is the spirit of love.

MAGICAL STATES

I am more than ever persuaded that all magical states, by which I mean states of mere illumination, however wonderful, terminate in Paradise or hell. But that this is not the true end seems clear, not only from the fact that Paul, who had been caught up into Paradise, did not regard it as an end; but still more [from] the fact that Christ, the Pattern of patterns, did not stay there, but came forth out of Paradise and hell by resurrection.

THE BAPTISM OF THE SPIRIT

As to your question, ' Is this baptism of the Spirit something apart and distinct from all that has gone before ? ' I answer, It is, I think, something 'distinct' but not 'apart' from it; by which I mean that it is a further experience, or a fuller measure of experience, in the same one life of Christ. Yet I could not say that it is 'apart' from what has gone before; for it grows out of, and is the crown of, what has preceded it; just as the bud or blossom in the plant is not apart from what has gone before, but is only the manifestation of the life which all along has been within. . . . Christ is the pattern of it all. The eternal life was in Him just as truly when He was an unborn Babe, or a Child of twelve years old, as when He was a full-grown Man at His baptism. But at His baptism He came experimentally, as Son of man, to a light and power which He had not known before; and still more was this the case at His resurrection. Yet at every stage His life was by the Holy Ghost; for it was by the Holy Ghost that He was at first conceived; it was by the Holy Ghost that He was baptised in Jordan ; and again it was by the Holy Ghost at His resurrection that He was declared to be the Son of God with power. All is by the Holy

Ghost; yet there are different measures, if one may say so, in the manifestation of this One Spirit. Just so is it when 'Christ is formed in us, the hope of glory;' for the life of the last Adam, as of the first, is re-enacted in all that are His, who therefore can say, 'Christ liveth in me.'   The Christian writers of bygone days, in speaking of all this, used to compare the stage before the baptism of the Spirit to that of espousal, that after it to the marriage union; so that, according to this view, the experience of the disciples as set before us in the Four Gospels, which is the first experience of Christian disciples, would be that of being espoused to Christ; that described in the Acts of the Apostles after Pentecost would be that of being united in marriage to Christ.   It is of little consequence how you speak of these stages.   But it is well, when we can bear it, to see that there are such stages—that there is, first, a separating stage; then, a purifying or illuminating one; and, last, a uniting stage. . . . Each stage is beautiful and perfect in its season; and it is a mistake to hurry. We do no good by making our children into little men or women, or by wishing to marry them too soon.

THE LORD WILL PROVIDE

It is now many, many years, not long after I married, since I and my dear wife offered ourselves and all that we had to be the Lord's. In a groaning world and a groaning Church it did not take many years to bring our little store far lower than would once have seemed enough for us. But from that day to this, though children have been given to us, and boys have had to be educated and started in life, I have never lacked any good thing, God always providing. If only some dear souls, who doubt some things in the Gospel, could but go through my path, and could see, as I have done, that giving to Christ and receiving from Him is a reality—far more real than dealing with the truest earthly friend—that He is not a dead but a living God—that He is really with us, really not only able but delighting (as I should delight) to help us when we are helpless and can do nothing—they would know what a Rock of Ages is under our feet.

REST IN THE LORD

Rest in the Lord. Rest in Him as you rest in your bed at night; with heart beating all the while, with lungs breathing all the while; yet casting yourself and your burden on that which you know will support you. So rest in the Lord; not without heart-exercise or without ceaseless prayer for those you love; knowing that underneath are the everlasting arms.

SEPARATE FROM SINNERS

What is the separateness of Christ? Having in my young days gone all lengths in outward separation—having been a Pharisee of the Pharisees, and by my example and ministry at a certain stage of my life led others into the same sort of outward separateness—having watched for their souls as one that must give account, and having seen what the tree is by the fruits it brought forth—and having since then by grace had opened to me what was and is the life of the true Son, who was holy, harmless, separate from sinners, but who yet took their place, and took their form, and took their curse and burden for them—[I see] . . . the difference between Christ's separateness and that of many who desire to follow Him.

CHRISTMAS

Many thanks for your kind Christmas greeting, which I heartily re-echo for you and all yours. God grant that this Christmas may be a Christmas to you all—a time for Christ really to come and dwell with

you, and that we may all show in our lives, what in
word we all confess, that God has indeed made our
nature His tabernacle, and dwells in us.   But now as
of old poor welcomes here await Him, for even when
we receive Him in our hearts there is so little room for
Him that He is laid away among thoughts and wishes
which are too often beast-like. So at least it has been
with me. We find room in our poor hearts for
almost any other guest—for the world, or for the things
of the world, which ask admission so importunately.
But for Christ there is no room in that poor inn. And
yet not for one moment does it alter His unchanging
purpose to bless us. If we have little room for Him,
His answer is, 'I have prepared My feast for you, and
yet there is room.' Room, not only for those who have
no room for Him, but for those who again and again
despise the provision which He has made for us
because He knows we need it.   But oh, the soul-
hunger such souls must one day waken up to, when,
without creatures, they find themselves also without
God.   For hearts are made for God.   All the things
which fill them, though they fill, can never satisfy.
But God satisfies.   Some of us have proved this.   All
must prove it.   And blessed will that hunger be, however painful its coming to some, which forces them at
last to cry for God.

UNQUENCHABLE FIRE

You ask, 'What is the work of the unquenchable fire after it has burnt up all the chaff?' I suppose it is to be the light and life of all things. . . . If, as St. Paul says, 'our God is a consuming fire,' inasmuch as He is eternal and everliving He must be an unquenched and unquenchable fire—a fire which burns up all that is corrupt, only to bring forth and quicken what shall be uncorrupt. . . . Even natural life, the life of this world, is fire, though it is a fire only lighted by and akin to the sun, the light of this world. All hellish life in like manner is only a fire of another kind, a fire which through God's mercy will, I believe, be quenched some day, but which is kindled or lighted, like all other fires, from the light of its own world, the light or sun of hell being only self-love. So heavenly life is fire also, fire kindled and lighted from the Sun of the heavenly world, Who is love; for 'God is love,' and, as David says, 'The Lord God is a sun.' To bring this heavenly fire and life of love into this world Christ came down; for He said, 'I am come to cast fire into the earth; and what do I desire but that it should be at once kindled?' And this heavenly fire, like the fires of earth and hell, depends on its own Sun, only that the Sun of heaven is eternal Love, Who will burn up all dross, and yet shine in and with those whom He has kindled with His own life for ever and ever. And we must, if we are to dwell in God, have a life which, because it is of the fire, can stand unhurt in it. For a natural man to dwell in God would be like my hand staying in a furnace. But God gives us a life which can abide in Him.

SPIRITISM

This, if I err not, is what is coming upon Christendom. Men will believe a lie if only it is confirmed or authenticated by a miracle. And they will have miracles enough. Spirits of devils are coming forth to work miracles. Awful trial surely for all. How awful for those who know not Christ!

1875

CHRIST'S LIVING BLOOD

The key to all this question of eating Christ's flesh and drinking His blood lies in the words, 'The blood is the life.' And the thing man wants is not a dying, human, earthly life, but an undying, Divine, and heavenly life. . . . To drink in a dying life, or dying blood, would never make man undying.

1876

THE SPIRIT AND THE CROSS

To my mind there is a most direct connection between N.'s general teaching and his last error. For he was so possessed with the one idea of the baptism of the Spirit that he could see nothing else, and often spoke as if souls could and ought at once to take a place beyond conflict, where their whole nature was so filled with the Spirit that it lost its innate proneness to sin, where struggling ceased, and where what he called the ' sabbath ' was come, and ' Canaan ' reached. The idea which lay at the foundation of this teaching, the idea of God possessing us, was a grand and true one, one which needs to be brought out especially among those who were resting too much in what they called justification by faith. But grand and true as the idea was, to be safely pressed it needed its proper complement, namely, the daily cross and daily death to old Adam, which indeed ever goes with the indwelling of the Spirit, but which is often practically overlooked by those who have only recently got hold of the blessed doctrine of that indwelling. Knowing, therefore, how this doctrine of the indwelling of the Spirit might be abused, and was almost certain to be abused, unless the daily cross, that is, a daily self-mortification, were also preached, and practically set forth in equal measure, I did what I could by calling attention to Job's experience, which witnessed what could come out of the perfect man if he were sufficiently tried; and then by the lesson taught also by the healings in Canaan on the sabbath day, which showed what wretched sicknesses cleaved to some in Israel who had reached Canaan and knew the sabbath rest; and still more by calling N.'s special attention to the awful fact that even after Satan was bound for a thousand years, the same Satan could and would be loosed for a little season. . . . This is always the peril of great ideas. They are only safe under a daily cross, or to a long-schooled or long-tried soul, who is carrying the burden either of poverty or pain or bereavement, or some daily rule of self-denial. Without these the soul is like a boat without ballast, upset even by a favourable wind; or like Noah, intoxicated even in a new world beyond the waters by his privileges. Noah's drunkenness has been repeated in the Church a thousand times. The very blood of the true Vine becomes his shame. For a grand idea is an idea which can turn men's heads. We do not become giddy by standing on a hassock or on a chair. It is standing on the top of the Monument

E

or of St. Paul's that upsets us. Some one says,
'A great idea, like a great hero, must slay its thousands.' Any great truth, therefore, has this peril,
that souls at first do not see that there is always some
equally great truth, which seems almost antagonistic to
the first, which is required to balance it. Here was
N.'s fall. No blame to the truth he held (which
nevertheless will be blamed), but only to the weakness
of him who taught it.

HUMILIATION AND EXALTATION

Of course you have noticed the way St. Paul
speaks of himself as he gets onward in his Christian
life. Writing to the Corinthians, in the year 59,
he is satisfied to say of himself that he is the
'least of the apostles.' Five or six years later,
in A.D. 64, writing to the Ephesians, he calls himself
'less than the least of all saints.' A year or two
later, and just before his death, writing to his beloved
Timothy, he puts himself among the 'sinners,' yea,
he confesses himself to be the chief of sinners for
whom Christ died. So he gets on, and is going up
when he seems to be going down; for God's way of
bringing up His children is to bring them down.
Indeed, this is the drift of all the 'Psalms of Degrees,'

or 'of the going up.'   One of the latest of them begins,
' Out of the deep have I cried to Thee, O Lord.'

THE OLD MAN MUST BE SLAIN

The 'evil man' and the 'violent man' and the
' enemy' whom the writer of Psalm lxix. would fain
see utterly overthrown is really the ' old man,' the
' carnal mind which is enmity with God,' . . . who must
be destroyed and brought to dissolution, that out of the
destruction the new creature may emerge in all its proper beauty.   Therefore it is written again and again in
the prophets (which so few understand in their spiritual
sense), that ' the Lord's sword shall go forth out of
its sheath against all flesh, that all flesh may know
that the Lord Himself has drawn this sword against
it ; nor shall this sword return to its sheath any more
(see Ezek. xxi. 4, 5).   And all this is done that
' every heart may melt, and all hands be feeble, and
every spirit faint, and all knees be weak : ' in other
words, that they may be brought into that state
where God can lift them up. . . . The Lord can no
more spare our earthly fallen nature than the priest
of old could spare the sacrifice which was brought to
him.

ONLY NEED REVEALS CHRIST

You say you think that 'the people who turn to
Christ because they are tired and disappointed will never
know Him best.'   But who ever turns to Him until
they want or need Him ?   And can He ever show
what He is except in supplying some need either of
head or heart ?   A mother, a physician, a friend, a
husband, is only known really as each supplies some
need.   All through the young days of the world, in
the old Greek, or Jewish, or Roman days, Christ was
never known as He has been since, simply because
human nature was younger and fresher and stronger,
and had not learnt, as it has since learnt, that all
flesh is grass.   As we need Christ, so we know Him.

1877

THE DISCIPLINE OF SELF-DESPAIR

In what you tell me of yourself, dark as it may
seem to you, I see marks of the experience of Christ ;
and therefore I feel sure that what is now dark to
you will all one day be light, even as I think I may
say it is already light to me.   For you speak now of
what you never seemed to feel or know—the utter

sifting and self-despair by which the Lord perfects
us. You tell me of the 'anguish of a long night of
involuntary doubt, if not of God, yet of His dealings
with you, which, after so many years of undivided
communion, was like being cast into a measureless
abyss, ever falling, and never ceasing to fall yet
deeper from God into darkness ; ' and you say, ' Why
this awful world of agony and suffering, so often pro-
portioned almost to the soul's utter devotion to God ?
Why, having committed the keeping of my soul to
God, was it suffered so terribly to mistake its way ?
Why bless and curse without measure the same
things ? ' In a word, Why, to use old John Newton's
well-known hymn, is prayer always answered by
crosses ? Read again and again his well-known
hymn, beginning,

> I asked the Lord that I might grow
> In faith, and love, and every grace,

and you will get the true answer, namely, that this
experience, so humbling, so trying, is the one only
appointed road, known by all the saints, testified of
throughout all Scripture, seen above all in Christ, the
perfect Pattern, yet rarely seen in the earlier stages of
the Christian life, but most sure to be known sooner
or later if ever we are to be conformed to Christ. It
was the lack of any reference in your ministry to this

sort of experience which made me, more than anything else, often tremble for you. For this self-
despair is the one only appointed way; and in the
way to this we are at times so tempted that we seem
almost to despair of God. You may, indeed, know
death and resurrection with Christ *by faith*, and
only sing triumphantly, as Moses and Israel sang
when they crossed the Red Sea. But you cannot
know this death and resurrection *in experience*, as
Israel knew it when they crossed Jordan, without
having, instead of a song, the pain and wound of circumcision, and the helplessness which such circumcision brings for a season, and this in the presence
of your enemies. Is it a mistake in Scripture that
there is no song after crossing Jordan, but instead of
it the painful circumcision of full-grown men—not
painful only, but for the time crippling? So in the
well-known passage in Isa. lxiv., where we have the
prophet's earnest cry that God would 'rend the
heavens and come down, that the mountains might
flow down at His presence'—a prayer which, I doubt
not, you have prayed—have you not noticed how it
is answered? The prophet immediately adds, 'When
Thou didst terrible things which we looked not for,
the mountains flowed down at Thy presence.' The
thing asked was granted; but how and when?

'When Thou didst terrible things which we looked not for.' We did not expect that the answer would come, and could only come, through such 'terrible things.' 'For,' as the prophet adds, 'from the beginning of the world men have not heard, nor perceived by the ear, neither hath the eye seen, O God, beside Thee, what Thou hast prepared for him that waiteth for Thee.' For we are all slow to learn that the Cross, or crossing of our will and nature, is the one only appointed way. For 'Thou meetest,' that is, comest in the opposite way to, 'him that worketh righteousness; those that remember Thee in their ways:' in a word, Thou seemest to cross and oppose them. See how St. Paul quotes this text in the passage where he speaks of Christ's Cross (1 Cor. ii. 2, 8, 9): 'They crucified the Lord of glory; for it never entered into the heart of man that those were the things which God had prepared for them that love Him. But God has by His Spirit revealed these things to us,' even that 'many are the troubles of the righteous.' But in spite of these words, and of all the testimony of the prophets, even 'disciples understand none of these things, and the saying is hid from them,' though it is repeated in their ears by One who is a true Cross-bearer (Luke xviii. 31-34). All showing that an open Bible is not an opened Bible, and that we only see what we have learned to see.

The fact is that the utter ruin and judgment of the flesh must be felt as well as believed before the true Spirit is fully given. Dispensationally this was shown in Judaism being utterly broken up before Pentecost. In our experience we have to prove the same thing. A fleshly form of the Spirit, indeed, there is before this ruin and judgment of the flesh is known; as when the Spirit came upon Samson and Jephthah, and they did mighty works. For, as there is a fleshly knowledge of Christ as well as a spiritual, so there is a fleshly knowledge of the Holy Ghost; but the outpouring of the Spirit of the Son, who says always 'Not My will,' comes only through the Cross; and the Cross is not the improvement or glorification of the old nature, but its entire judgment and dissolution. The lack of a distinct utterance on this point I always noticed in your teaching. You spoke often of the Spirit and of the transports of true joy, but rarely of the 'much tribulation,' or 'threshing' (for 'tribulation' means only 'threshing'), which was and is the road to it; rarely of the anguish, the shame, the humiliation, which is ever brought by the consuming fire we long for, and which is the one unfailing prelude to the transfiguration of the sacrifice

in all the true elect. Of course, visions and transports and catching up into the third heaven, may be
all right ; yea, they are all, if true visions and true
transports, truly blessed ; though when they are so
they always bring with them 'thorns in the flesh and
messengers of Satan, lest we should be exalted above
measure.' But visions and transports without such
balance, and without a daily Cross, are not, as it
seems to me, the royal road. The Cross is the one
true token—do we suffer ? Where this is we are safe
—where, crossed in our will and service again and
again, we say, 'Not my will, but Thy will.' Often,
therefore, did I feel a sort of tremor come over me
while I listened to you ; for I felt what a shaking
there might be from the foundations. Yet, knowing
the goodness of the Lord, I was assured all would
be right ; and all will be right, and what is now dark
will one day be perfect light.

In one word, dear brother, 'the life of Jesus' is
all, and the life of Jesus is a tempted, suffering life.
It is the life of a 'man of sorrows and acquainted
with grief ; ' the life of One 'despised and rejected of
men ; ' the life of One 'numbered with the trans-
gressors,' whom men 'esteemed stricken, smitten of
God, and afflicted ; ' yea, the life of One whom 'it
pleased the Lord to bruise ; ' a life which yet is kept

in perfect peace, though it may, and must, in a certain hour cry out, 'My God, why hast Thou forsaken Me?' Thank God, I have known something of this life. You, too, have prayed to manifest this 'life of Jesus.' How is it to be done? Paul says, 'We are troubled on every side, but not perplexed; we are cast down, but not destroyed: always bearing about in the body the dying of the Lord, that the life also of Jesus might be made manifest in our body.' There is no other way to manifest this life but by a daily death and cross. Let us not stumble at the royal road. But, indeed, all disciples first stumble at the Cross. . . .

I may perhaps help you if I say that, in sifting trial, the one safe way is not to write or speak at all except to God; for God speaks for those who do not justify themselves. And we cannot, even in the most righteous way, justify ourselves without losing some blessing. . . . God can, and will, justify you in due time, and give you back all and more than all that has been lost, even all the days and years which the locust and the cankerworm have eaten.

DOUBTS

To speak more directly as to your doubts touching revealed religion, I suppose a man (I do not say a woman) will always be open to some such doubts until

he has himself seen and experienced the very things
which revealed religion speaks of. But all may see
those very things, if only Christ is formed and grows up
in us. We are not left to hearsays or tradition, which
may be corrupted, or to a mere letter or book, which
may be a fable or which cannot be understood.
What God has given us is an eternal life. Christ and
His saints had it of old. We have, or may have, the
very selfsame life at this day. Till we have it, and
have it in its fullness, there must be more or less
uncertainty. But the Gospels not only tell me what
happened 1,800 years ago. That would be but little
help to me. They tell me what I see and feel; and
I really see no further into the Gospels, or into
Scripture generally, than I see the selfsame things
now done or doing by the same one blessed Worker,
who is still with and amongst us, though few see Him,
and fewer understand Him. Thus the truly converted
man is himself not only the comment but also the
fulfilment of all Scripture; for it all speaks of but
two things, namely, the old man and the new; and
both these are in us, and still go on their old way, as
unchangeably as vines and brambles now grow exactly
as they did four thousand years ago. Nothing but
the formation of Christ in us, His conception, birth,
life, death, and resurrection—that is, the fulfilment

in us of all that we read in Scripture was fulfilled for
us—can ever perfectly free us from such doubts as
those you speak of.

MEDIATION

The question which you asked . . . has more
than once come back to me, as to the needs-be for
some one to represent man to God, or, as the apostle
puts it, to 'appear in the presence of God for man,' as
well as to represent God to man, or, in other words,
to appear in the presence of man for God. . . . The
illustration given by Claude St. Martin, or in his
correspondence, came to my mind. It is this, and
I think it meets your inquiry. Suppose we want to
introduce to each other, or rather to bring together,
two substances which are naturally too far apart or too
dissimilar to unite, what must we do? How can the
union be effected? Chemistry teaches us that it can
be done by adding or bringing in a third substance,
which has affinities with the other two. Thus, for
instance, if we would unite oil and water, we must
add a fixed alkali, when the water and oil will combine
intimately. Here we have a natural, and therefore
a Divine, type of the intermediate agents, such as the
priest or the apostle, who are needed to introduce and
unite God to man and man to God, the first of whom,

that is the priest, brings man to God, just as the other, that is the apostle, brings God to man: in either case the union being accomplished by an agent who participates in and also assimilates with the natures of the beings they have to bring together.

'THE MIGHT OF SACRAMENTAL GRACE'

Touching the expression of your bishop which you refer to, 'the might of sacramental grace,' which you say is 'Dutch to you,' I could say much if I had time. I believe in 'the might of sacramental grace.' Truth, the truth of God, can only come to fallen creatures sacramentally, that is, by sensible *media* or mediums connected with the senses, which are channels by which the truth of God, which has all power, gets into us. The Word of God, the eternal Son, by Whom all things were created, and in Whom all things consist, is much nearer to all men than any man or means of grace outside of them can be, for in Him they live and move and have their being; and yet, such is our fall out of the spirit-world into outward things, that is the things of sense, that He in Whom we live can only get at us at first from the outside. The Word is nigh us; but to be heard, it has to come to us first through the senses—either by preaching, addressed to the sense of hearing, or by acted words, commonly called sacraments, addressed to the sense of sight. In both, whether in preaching or in sacraments, God tries to speak to us. In the one He speaks to our ears, in the other to our eyes. For, when we are very little babes, words addressed to our ears are not enough : we want something which speaks to our eyes also. Therefore parents smile and nod at their babes, the smiles and nods being acted words, or sacraments, meaning and saying, 'I love you.' Therefore in speaking to the deaf and dumb you must speak by your fingers. . . . That this should be needed shows how fallen we are. But that it is needed is a fact ; and a fact which God meets by giving His Word in a creature-form, which thus reaches man from without.

Now, all this, imperfectly as I have expressed it, shows the needs-be for sacraments or sense-mediums for communicating truth to fallen man ; but what I have said does not touch the 'might' of these sacramental mediums, or 'the might of sacramental grace,' which you say is 'Dutch to you.' Yet these mediums, creaturely as they are and acting through the senses, are divinely mighty. You, with your early training and your present views, doubt this as respects the acted words, which are generally called sacraments, in which, by some outward act, as by dipping a person in water, and raising him out of it again in the Name

of the Father and of the Son and of the Holy Ghost,
you witness or teach that man is by nature dead—
therefore you bury him—but that in the place of
death, even in the grave (for we are 'buried in
baptism'), God meets him with life, because His
Name is Father, Son, and Holy Ghost—you, I say,
with your present and probably inherited view of
sacraments, doubt whether there is 'might' in them.
Yet you believe that there is 'might' in preaching
by word of mouth.   But preaching by act may be just
as efficacious.   At all events, preaching by word of
mouth, or by spoken words, is really just as sacramental as the acted words which are more commonly
called sacraments; for, as I have already said, when
you preach you are simply getting at the soul by the
sense of hearing, through the vibrations in the air
made by the movements of your tongue, all which is
physical and sensible; and, further, when you so
preach, the 'might' or power which goes forth, and
gets into the soul, far transcends any intellectual
apprehension of what is said.   Take as an example
the words, 'The blood of Jesus Christ His Son
cleanseth us from all sin.'   Souls get a blessing from
these words who, if asked to explain them, will, in nine-
teen cases out of twenty, certainly give you an entirely
wrong explanation of them.   And yet the words are a

real blessing to them ; just as baptism and the Lord's
Supper are blessings to those whose explanation of
these acted words is wholly wrong. Ask your truest
converts to explain what blood of Christ cleanseth, and
how it cleanses them, or touches their sin, and see
how utterly ignorant and wrong they are, first, as to
whether it is the literal physical blood which was
shed on Calvary that cleanses, and, secondly, how
this outward blood has ever touched them ; or, if it is
not this outward blood, what blood it is. Yet the
words have ' might,' and the might in them is the
' might of sacramental grace.'

CONFORMITY TO CHRIST

God's will is that we should be ' conformed to the
image of His dear Son ; ' and even while we are here,
if with open face we will behold as in a glass the
glory of the Lord, we may be changed into the same
image, from glory to glory, as by the Spirit of the
Lord. . . . Not only may we be conformed to Christ's
sufferings and death while we are here, but further we
may also surely know the power of His resurrection,
and even here attain to that resurrection from among
the dead which Paul so earnestly prayed for. . . . The
work has all already been wrought *for us* in the Person
of our Lord Jesus Christ ; but that which has been

wrought *for us* in Him is all to be wrought *in us* by
Him, so that as He is so may we be even in this
world.   For 'Jesus Christ is of God made unto us
wisdom, even righteousness, and sanctification, and
redemption.' . . . But though all these three blessings
are ours *in* Christ, we do not personally experience
them except as we look for them and expect them and
wait for them *from* Christ.   Till we feel that we want
righteousness, though all righteousness is laid up for
us in Christ, we do not draw it out of Him.   Then,
having obtained righteousness, till we feel that we want
sanctification, though all measures of holiness are laid
up for us in Christ, we do not draw them out of Him
for our joy and God's glory.   And so again, having
obtained sanctification from Christ, till we feel that we
need redemption, that is, the redemption of the body,
though this too is laid up for us in Christ, we do not
receive it, simply because we do not look for it and expect it and wait for it from Him.   For He is able to
change, and will one day change, these vile bodies;
but will He change any who are not looking to Him
to be changed? . . . As Paul says to the Philippians,
it is only as many as be, or wish to be, perfect who
can be thus minded, or have these thoughts.   To
others, such thoughts seem merely dreams or imagination; as if any of us could possibly imagine a higher

F

or better destiny for ourselves than God our Father
has in store for us.   But the way to this is not in
seeking visions or transports or great things for ourselves, but in meekly and humbly every day taking
up our daily cross and humbling ourselves, knowing
that when we come down into Jordan with Christ
then heaven opens to us, and when we die to our
own will, and say in all, 'Thy will be done,' then
from the cross and grave and apparent defeat of all
our hopes, not in our own strength, nor in selfhood,
but in the power of God, we are raised up as from the
dead to live and walk in God.

Of course, in this state, as it was with Christ, so
will it be with us.   'The world seeth Me no more,
but ye see Me.'   In resurrection we can only deal
with quickened or converted souls, even as Christ
after His resurrection only appeared to disciples ; but
through them we may reach many more.   We seem
to be useless—the world thinks we are dead—the
worldly, carnal Church thinks with the world.   Yet
the life of Christ through death is even stronger than
before, and will rule and subdue and bless all.   Thus
the veil rent *for* us in Christ has to be rent *in* us also
with Christ.   I know it is so, and I think you will
know this also.

1878

THE FIRST CREATION, OUT OF LIGHT

Did God originally bring life out of death and division, or life out of life? Was His first creation a creation arising out of confusion and imperfection, or out of His own fullness and perfection? Is not matter itself a state of fall, and a fallen form of spirit? The analogy you refer to, of the conception, growth, and birth of man, is all resurrection, for the womb is the grave, and is always so regarded in the typical language of Holy Scripture. Was the grave the beginning? Certainly all present nature advances, as you say, from imperfection to perfection. But present nature is fallen. Was this the law of God's unfallen creation? Did He first begin to work on darkness, division, and disorder; or did He not bring forth life out of perfect life? Was the first man, wherever he was created, formed through all the stages you refer to, or was he brought forth a God out of God?

THE EUCHARISTIC SACRIFICE

Your view of the Eucharistic Sacrifice is this, that 'it is our sacrifice, the entire surrender of self, the pouring out of our lives as a sweet savour of praise and love to God.' Do High Churchmen deny this? Not one of them. They, quite as much as you, say, 'Here we offer and present unto Thee, O Lord, ourselves, our souls and bodies, to be a reasonable, holy, and acceptable sacrifice unto Thee;' while their life is certainly not less of a sacrifice for others than that of their Low Church brethren. But (and here High Churchmen differ from you) in addition to this view of our sacrifice they see in the Lord's Supper Christ's sacrifice—that He is ever pouring out His blood, that is, His life, for us, that we may take it in and drink it; and that He is ever giving His body, that is, His very Divine nature and substance, that we may feed upon it, and so be built up in the same nature. In a word, while you look upon Christ's sacrifice as a merely temporal act, and therefore past, a thing once done and ended eighteen hundred years ago, they look upon it (just as they look upon the generation of the Son and the Procession of the Spirit) as an eternal, and therefore ever-present, thing, still continuing, as long as we need His substance and life to build up and sustain His life in us. And all the misapprehensions or contradictions which they may mix up with this true view, that Christ is yet giving Himself for us, and that therefore He is still sacrificing Himself, cannot and do not nullify or take away the real blessing which this view of Christ still giving Himself to be our Life must communicate to every needy, hungry, wanting heart. Your view of the Eucharistic Sacrifice, that it is only our sacrifice of ourselves, does not meet the heart's full need. With all his mistakes, the High Churchman in all this is contending for a truth which you and your pamphlet wholly overlook.

And Christ's words at the Institution of the Supper show that He did not look upon it as only expressing our sacrifice of self, but, much more, His own sacrifice, a sacrifice which is eternal, that is, ever-present. For He said, as He sat with His disciples, and before what you would call His blood-shedding, 'This is My blood, which is being poured out for you.' Must it not still be poured out, if it is true that we are to 'drink it;' and that 'except we drink it, we have no life in us'? And must not His body still be given, if we are to 'take and eat it,' as He said, 'He that eateth Me, even he shall live by Me'? And if this blood is still poured out for us to drink, and if this flesh is still given us to eat, is not this most literally and truly a sacrifice of Christ?

The fact is, the Ritualist whom you judge really believes that he wants Christ's body and blood as the

very food which supports his new life, and that
Christ really gives this flesh and blood to him ; and
though his explanation of how this is done may be
incorrect, he nevertheless comes to Christ desiring to
take in that promised 'flesh and blood,' that is, the
substance and life which shall build up and keep alive
the new life in him. His doctrine of the Eucharistic
Sacrifice, therefore, is that Christ yet pours out
or gives His blood, and that the sacrament is a
'memorial' of this, a memorial of that body and
blood which the Lord gave and is giving for us.
Your doctrine of the Eucharistic Sacrifice is that it
is only a sacrifice and surrender of yourself, and a
memorial of a past act of Christ, which indeed healed
the breach between God and man in Christ, but which
was ended eighteen hundred years ago.

PAST AND PRESENT

You say that, because Scripture speaks of Christ's
sacrifice as an accomplished thing, therefore it cannot
go on, and therefore Christ cannot yet be pouring out
His blood for us, to give it us to drink. This is an
apparent contradiction which necessarily cleaves to all
our first conceptions of the facts of our redemption,
because our redemption is an eternal thing. But
Scripture does not hesitate to accept the apparent

contradiction, for only thus can it express the blessed fact. Thus we read, 'Ye are dead, and risen with Christ;' 'Ye have put off the old man with his deeds, and have put on the new;' 'Put on, therefore, as the elect of God, bowels of mercies, . . . and put off all these, anger, wrath, malice, blasphemy' (see Col. iii. 1–12). The New Testament is full of this, and must be. So, though 'Christ once suffered for sins,' and 'in that He died, He died unto sin once,' He is still 'crucified afresh, and put to an open shame' by those who yet call themselves His people.

THE JUDGMENT OF THE CHURCH

Sad as it is to hear of dear Carter being worried by Lord Penzance, it may be better for the Church than that smaller and less respected men should be assailed. For, if Carter is attacked or suspended, even the bishops may wake up to ask what it all means. Still, the end to me is quite clear. It is the old story of Israel once again. The fourth great form of Gentile or worldly power will certainly crush and sweep away the priesthood and the temple. For the Church's sins this must come at last. But the Church's judgment and failure, like Israel's, are but the prelude to a wider blessing . . . not for the elect only, but for all. Aaron's priesthood, with its threefold

order and temple, was great : Melchisedek's, without
temple, was greater still.   Consider how great this
man was, to whom Abraham, and Levi and Aaron in
Abraham, paid tithes.   The one is the priesthood of
the elect ; the other is the priesthood of man—a
truth which, as St. Paul says to the Hebrews, even
yet can hardly be spoken of without danger.   Both
priesthoods are fulfilled in Christ ; though what the
Church has ever gloried in has really been Aaron's
order, not Melchisedek's. . . . The fourth and last
form of Gentile power, with its S.P.Q.R., that is, the
assertion of the will of the people, will be the instru-
ment for shaking and sweeping away all that can be
shaken.   And the heaven must be shaken, that is,
the Church ; yea, it must be rolled up and depart as
a scroll, to bring in the full final redemption.   My
heart aches when I think of the anguish of those who,
like Israel of old, assured that what has been dispensed
to them has come from God, will fight to the bitter
end to save what is already doomed.   We have not
felt sufficiently for the difficulties of the high priests
of old, when a new ministry and a new dispensation
and a wider priesthood came upon them.   We may
have, we shall surely have, the same trial.   But how
many of the priests of Aaron's line, like John the
Baptist, are prepared to welcome the coming truth,

which lays the axe to the root of what is now standing ?

I did not think to write all this. But it has been upon my spirit for years and years. And I feel assured that it is true. What the Church now wants is prophetic light—light, that is, to know God's present will, His will as to existing things—whether this is 'a time to build' or 'a time to throw down.' No study of the letter of the dispensation will give this. No study of the old law would have shown that in Hezekiah's day the right thing was to 'defend Jerusalem ;' in Zedekiah's, to forsake it and 'fall to, the Chaldeans ;' and in a still later day to 'flee to the mountains.' No mere letter of the Gospel will show the Church's real need to-day. Direct prophetic light is needed—men to whom the Word of the Lord yet comes expressly. And yet these are the men whom the Church always rejects.

1879

MOVING FROM ONE SECTION OF THE CHURCH TO ANOTHER

The worst of going from one section of the Church to another is that, in so doing, souls generally are taken up with the points in which they differ from other Christians rather than with that common ruin and common salvation in which they all are one, which last, surely, is catholicity.

THE THREE WAYS

The dear old saints of bygone days used to map out the road as consisting in the main of three very distinct stages—first, the purgative way, when the soul is mainly occupied with the question of purification from sin, first from its guilt, and then also from, its indwelling power. All this is the first stage. Then comes the illuminative way, answering to the last half of the Six Days' work, when the soul is being furnished with gifts and light and power, not only to be blessed itself, but to be made a living blessing to all around. Lastly comes the unitive way, figured by the Seventh Day's rest, without an evening, when the creature's will has in all things been made one with God, when we come indeed to fellowship with the Father and with His Son, even to the Communion of the Holy Ghost, in which God can rest in us, and we in Him. These stages run into each other, but the dear old saints were right in speaking of this growth.

JOB AND DAVID

As to Job and David, I cannot add much to what you say. The one is the man that was 'perfect and upright,' with all sorts of gifts and blessings for a while entrusted to him; but this perfect man had not as yet been delivered from himself. With all his perfectness, self was still strong. So he says, 'When the ear heard *me*, then it blessed *me*; and when the eye saw *me*, then it gave witness to *me*; because *I* delivered the poor, and *I* caused the widow's heart to sing with joy; and *I* was eyes to the blind, and feet was *I* to the lame;' and so on, at very great length, all about *me* and *I*; till, like the veriest sinner, he is brought by losses and sorrows to find he needs not gifts and blessings only, but a living, loving God; when instead of saying, 'When the eye saw me,' he cries out, 'Now mine eye seeth *Thee*; therefore I abhor myself, and repent in dust and ashes.' And when he is brought to this, all is well again, ten times better than it was before. He has been emptied, to be filled with better things. Compare David and his Psalms with all this. In them you find the cries and songs of one who is anything but a perfect man. David had fallen into more than one very grievous sin; but through all, his hope was still in God. God was everything to him, and he himself in his own eyes was nothing. ' I am even as a beast before Thee: nevertheless, Thou hast holden me by my right hand. Thou shalt guide me with Thy counsel, and afterward receive me to glory. Whom have I in heaven but Thee ; and what is there upon earth that I desire like Thee ? The Lord is my rock, and my fortress, and my deliverer, and my God, my strength, my buckler, and the horn of my salvation.' In a word, in David, God is all. His wretchedness is the vessel for God's fullness. This is what we have to be brought to, if we would sing as we are called to sing and rejoice and give thanks, come what will within us or around us.

1880

THE SPIRIT OF MAN, AND THE FALL

The difference between us seems to be this. According to your view, man as man, fallen as he is, is regarded as having in, and as part of, his nature all he needs ; because his spirit is a son of God, which neither can sin nor die ; though his soul, which is the body of his spirit, has died and fallen.

According to my view, man, though a son of God,

has had his proper life poisoned by the false word, and so has died in spirit, soul, and body, and is therefore a dead and fallen son of God; who needs God's life to be raised up in him, though he is a son of God. And my view is that the renewal of the Divine life in him is the result, not of his spirit having remained unfallen, and so by its innate power overcoming his fallen psychical and bodily life, but of the incoming of the Word of God, in whom is life, whose incoming gives God's life and power to man's dead spirit, and hence to his soul and body in due season. And I believe that in the process of man's regeneration the working of the Word is first in man's spirit, then in his soul, and lastly in his body.

Of course I believe that, through grace, there is in all an inspoken Word of God in Whom is life, and in virtue of Whom the Divine life is requickened in our nature. This inspoken Word, if I am right, came with the Promise immediately after the Fall.

Where we differ is, that you think man's spirit is the Seed of God, and that this human spirit could not and did not die. I believe that the Divine Word is the Seed of God, which requickens the spirit which was slain and poisoned by the serpent's lie, and so makes man again a living son of God.

You argue that the words, ' Whatsoever is born of

God cannot commit sin,' prove that a son of God can neither fall nor die; and that therefore the Divine life has never died in man. If this be so, I do not understand the possibility of any fall, or the entrance of sin at all, among the sons of God. To say nothing of the devil, who abode not in the truth and fell, and who was a son of God, Adam at least was a son of God, and yet sinned and died. . . .

My belief is that the Fall began in the spiritual world, and that it is because spirit fell that we have matter as it now is : in other words, that the present state of matter is a sign and witness of the fall of certain spirits, who, I believe, will one day be restored.

There are other subordinate points in your letter which are full of interest ; as, for instance, man's being placed by God to subdue the earth, which you regard as describing what was ordained for man's own progress and advancement, but which, according to my view, speaks rather of his relation to another prior creation or family of sons of God who fell, into whose place man has been brought, ultimately to save those who preceded him, that is, the devil and his angels.

THE RUIN OF THE CHURCH

As to the E.C.U., I have of late been strongly tempted to join it ; for the assumption of the lay courts to alter, first direct Church doctrine, as in the Gorham case, and now ritual, seems to me simply monstrous. Could anything be more ridiculous than Mr. Justice Manisty's remarks the other day, when he gave judgment on Mr. Dale, as to the duty of Ritualists leaving the Church ? But spite of all this I cannot join the E.C.U., for I think I see distinctly that it is God's own purpose to overthrow the Church, even as it was His will to overthrow Jerusalem of old, when her time had come. There is a time when the Holy City is called Egypt; when our Lord is crucified in it; and I think I already see the last plague of Egypt, namely the smiting of the first-born ; for priests and kings are being smitten everywhere throughout Christendom. Of course this is a question involving prophetic light; for at one stage, in Hezekiah's day, the command is to ' stand by Jerusalem and to defend it ; ' at another stage, in Zedekiah's day, it is to ' fall to the Chaldeans,' that is, to go out and submit to them ; while later on, when the end is at hand, it is, ' then let them which are in Judea flee to the mountains.' This is when ' the

abomination which maketh desolate is seen to stand
in the holy place.' For a time comes when the Lord
does nothing to save Israel as a dispensation, though
to the end and ever He must heal all sickness and
disease and die for all, because He loves all. But
when the end has come, He leaves others like Barabbas
to fight against the Romans ; only bidding those who
follow Him, when a certain evil comes, to ' flee to
the mountains.' Those ' mountains ' are the high
ground of promise, for Canaan is the ground or land
of promise. There are two whole chapters about
these mountains in Ezekiel (chaps. xxxv. and
xxxvi.), all of which in their spiritual sense apply to
us who by grace ' inherit the promises.' The city
and temple must fall, fall at least on earth, like
Christ's body, which must be slain to overcome all
things. The truth will not fail, but the vessel in
which it has been contained is judged because of sin.
I may not be able to express for others what I see.
Certainly I could not express it in a hasty note. But
what I have said or hinted is my reason for not doing
what nature in me would like to do, by joining the
E.C.U., against the fourth and last great form of
Gentile power, namely the Roman, whose ensign, now
as of old, is S.P.Q.R., the P. or *populus* being the
mainspring, and ending in lawlessness which breaks

and tramples on every other form of power, till it is
at last headed up in the lawless one, whom the Lord
shall consume with the brightness of His coming.

But the Church has brought this on herself.
When I think what the Church has done—I am not
now thinking only of our English Church—when I
think what even our English Church has done, with
her Act of Uniformity, with its ' unfeigned assent and
consent,' and oath of the Queen's supremacy in
spiritual things—how she has by this made thousands
of dissenters, and made me a stranger to my brethren,
for I could not take the oath, and therefore could
not take priest's orders, when I felt an inward call to
minister—when I think of all the sins of the last
three hundred years, and the State-subserviency of
the bishops, though there have been exceptions—I
do not wonder at anything which may come as judgment on that which was set here to be God's chosen
witness. But I have written more than enough on this
sad subject. Thank God, out of all our ruin God will
bring better things. And first or last, let things
around be dark as they may, there will always be
room for faithful service and its reward.

G

THE FAILURE AND RESTORATION OF THE CHURCH

How I feel with you about the Church's state—how it has touched me in years past, till I hardly knew where I might not go. Now I see that all are equally fallen, all broken, all in one common shame, and that the remedy will not be in restoring or uniting the old thing, but in bringing in the new, which, like Christianity from Judaism, will be a stem out of the old rod, ever in it, yet to shine out more gloriously.

AARON AND MELCHISEDEK

We considered Christ as the substance of the Aaronic priesthood and sacrifice, in the tabernacle with outer and inner courts, and with a veil which is now rent, and with the blood to be taken even into the Holiest. But all this is not the priesthood after the order of Melchisedek, though the same One Blessed Lord is the substance of both. He fulfils both. Melchisedek's priesthood is not for sinners, as Aaron's was, but to bless him who had received the promises ; and so its main feature is benediction—benediction of the elect. It has nothing to do with inner or outer courts, or with blood, or with all those things which the Book of Leviticus so fully brings before us.

SACRAMENTAL CONFESSION

I must write you one line, not only to thank you for your pamphlet, but to say how thoroughly I go with it and with you from end to end. The only point—which, by the way, you have not touched—on which .I might differ with you, would be the question of *habitual* confession to a priest at *stated times*. If confession were a thing of the head, not of the heart, there would be less peril about this. But the confession is of the heart, that is, of the woman in us. Women must, of course, uncover themselves at times before their medical advisers. But to be always doing this, or to be habitually and constantly running to a doctor, as often as they feel themselves unwell, is surely not the way either to modesty or settled health. It impairs that proper shame which is Divinely implanted in our nature, and, further, appears to me to tend directly to increase weakness. Exercise and good food are better remedies. I speak here, of course, of spiritual exercise and spiritual food, as the best remedies for common soul-sickness, better as a rule than fifty doctors, or than one, though there are occasions when the heart must uncover itself.

1881

THE BODY AND THE RESURRECTION

The body answers to the soul's wants, being the soul's wife, the soul's friend, the soul's house, the soul's office, the soul's universe, being shapen into usefulness by the soul's ministrations. Some live in their bodies as savages would probably live if suddenly introduced into Buckingham Palace, with little or no knowledge of the use of the things they see and have on every hand, understanding nothing of the use of tables and chairs or knives and forks or baths or towels. It seems to me that the house in which we dwell at present is not the true body, but only a temporary house suited to the present state of the soul, which, as diseased and fallen, ... is disciplined by the house in which for a season it is called to sojourn; but that a new and better house even now is forming within us, growing from and around the grace of the new life quickened by the Word : which new house when complete will be the resurrection body. . . . The resurrection body is not a resurrection of relics, but a spiritual thing which grows from the new life implanted through Christ. I do not think it is put on *ab extra*, as a cloak upon a naked man, but is the covering rather which life forms for itself, as the life in a tree forms its body and clothes itself with leaves and buds, which break out from within. My belief is that matter is itself full of spirit, and can go back into spirit—it is the woman (*mater* or *matière*) who for a season, like Eve, is taken out of the man. The woman is the glory of the man, fallen and divided as she is, and destined some day to come back into the primeval union. But the very division brings things into manifestation which to some eyes would otherwise be unseen. I should therefore say that the body is the house and δόξα of the soul, as the soul is the δόξα of the spirit. The woman is the glory of the man, but the man is the glory of God. While masculine in relation to the woman, man is, or should be, feminine in relation to God. So it is, I think, with spirit, soul, and body.

PRAYERS FOR THE DEPARTED

I am glad to see the reference you make . . . to intercessory prayer for the departed. It is now eight-and-twenty years since the loss of one very near and dear to me led me to begin this practice. All increase of light has shown me that this is not mere natural affection. If Protestantism were not as blind as it is, it would have had eyes to see this long ago.

DEATH THE WAY OF DELIVERANCE

Death for sinners is the only way out of the dark world into which, through sin, man's soul is fallen— a lesson sealed to the Church by the two baptisms, of water and of fire, both of which seem to me to show the reason for the Second Death. For death, whether the first or second, though in one aspect it is judgment and destruction, in another (as baptism shows) is the one and only way of deliverance, for only 'he that is dead is freed from sin.' The wicked go out of this world with the hellish life of selfhood still unslain in them. Though dead to the life of the body, they . . . are not yet dead to, or delivered from, the dark world or 'power of darkness.' At the death of their present bodies their souls are yet in it; though for a while, like a babe born into this world, they may not fully know the awfulness of the world into which they have entered. What is the one only possible way out of it for them? Simply death. Therefore God's judgment and the Second Death. For God and Christ change not. It is all one plan— one way—the 'one baptism for the remission of sins:' carried out here and now in the elect, who will here live and die with Christ: to be carried out in due time in all, I believe, for all are redeemed in Christ:

but only carried out, whether in Christ or in the elect or in the so-called lost, through the same one process of 'the waters and the fires.'

SUFFERING AND SACRIFICE

This letter of yours, telling me what you are trying to do for poor X., has touched me much. She is indeed a sufferer; but in cases like hers (and I have known more than one) I think those who try to help the sufferer are more pained and hurt even than the sufferer herself. Certainly, to help any, you must bear their pains and sorrows for them; and the higher sympathy and tenderness, which is in the hearts of those that help, makes their pain often greater and keener than the pains of those to whom they minister. . . . She is, as Dr. E. here told her, a mass of disease; and as far as earthly remedies go she is almost beyond help. . . . Such cases have greatly tried me in former years, when I have cried to the Lord for help for those who are beyond the reach of earthly help. But the Lord has allowed some to suffer on without apparent alleviation for many years. I feel sure that in all such cases the Lord by the suffering is doing far more than any of us know. He may, by the suffering, be serving even souls in another world. They may possibly see what their sins have done to those they love, and this may bring on a repentance not to be repented of. The suffering, too, may actually serve other members of the Church here. Disease in the body always fixes on and comes out in the weakest members, and its so coming out relieves the rest of the body. I think it is so in the Body, the Church. Its sickness settles on the weaker members, and comes out in them; and naturally by this suffering others may be freed from what otherwise would touch them. All suffering is in one aspect sacrificial, even if it is penal, as in the case of the Sin and Trespass Offerings; and poor dear X. by her pains may be relieving others. Certainly, she is a member of the Body of which Christ is the Head, and she suffers, and you suffer with her, even as I too have suffered to see her. Can all this suffering of those very near and dear to Christ be without some good fruit? Only let us cast her and ourselves more and more upon God, and give up our will to Him, saying, 'Father, if it is Thy will that this suffering should continue awhile, by it fulfil Thine own purpose.' Then there must be blessed fruit of the suffering. I feel that there are some evils which for a while are permitted, to the glory of God. It is a mistake to think that they are to be removed at once. Some day they will be removed. The day is coming when there will be no more crying and tears. But they are permitted for a while. Has not Christ all power in heaven and earth? yet He permits them. Only let us cast ourselves and our dear ones on the Lord, not over-anxious even respecting the greatest pain. The time is short. Let those who weep be as though they wept not. The burden is not yours, but Christ's. Do you not know how, even with the best intentions, we may be attempting what the Lord has never laid upon us? At first we do all from self for self. Then the stage comes when we do much from self for Christ. At last we reach the rest, to do all from Christ for Christ and His creatures. The proof that we are doing things from self for Christ is that we undertake what is beyond us. We say, 'There is no one else to do this, therefore I must do it; but it is too much for me.' I hardly think a soul can say this who only does all from Christ for Christ. He does not lay upon us more than we can bear; though I know He often lays a Cross upon us, the fruit of the sins of others, it may be, under which we seem to fall. Yet the heart may be at rest under it all. The Lord give you this heart-rest in this sad case. And may His grace be sufficient for you.

REALITY OF THE NEW MAN

One thing is quite clear to me, that Christ *in* us is as real as Christ *for* us. The New Man in me or in you, and the new birth, and the new life, to me are no figures of speech, but the most real of all things ; the outward man, and the outward birth and life, to me being the phenomenal, and only shadows of the true.

SEERS AND CRITICS

As the old saw has it, ' Truth may be blamed, but cannot be shamed.' It may, and will, be crucified, but it must rise again. Every true word once spoken is stronger than all the reviews . . . if they only repeat some mere tradition of men. Meanwhile, the seers for a season are all ' stones which the builders disallow.' Do not, therefore, be surprised if your book is abused. As Wendell Holmes says, Every true thought on every real subject knocks the breath out of somebody. You may be sure you have said nothing of much consequence if no one finds any fault with what you say.

LITTLE CHILDREN

What is it to become ' like a child' ? Little children are very foolish, and often very wilful. But there is one thing a little child never does—it never thinks about its own safety. It never says, ' I wonder who will bolt the door to-night, or who will get me the milk for to-morrow's breakfast.' It always trusts its father. Be a little child. Give up questions, and rest in the Lord.

1882

FAITH, HOPE, AND LOVE IN GOD

I write a line at once in answer to your friendly critic's remonstrance with you as to Faith, Hope, and Charity being in God. Whoever your critic is, if he denies this, he is wrong. The first thing, if I remember right, which set me thinking on this matter was the fact (alluded to in the note on p. 250 of my ' Types of Genesis ') that the early Fathers, Ambrose, Augustine, and others, while they distinctly teach that Abraham, Isaac, and Jacob are types of the life of Faith, Hope, and Charity respectively in the believer, no less distinctly say that the same Abraham, Isaac, and Jacob are types of the Father, the Son, and the Holy Ghost. . . . Further, if our life as believers, sons, and servants of God is the Divine Life, and if our life is one of Faith, Hope, and

Charity, must it not follow that Faith, Hope, and
Charity are parts of the Divine Life, that is, the Life
of God? So long as we are without His Life, we
are without Faith, Hope, and Charity. Just as His
Life grows in us, Faith, Hope and Charity grow likewise, and grow simply because He lives in us. And
St. Paul's words as to Abraham's faith (Rom. iv. 17),
that it was '*like unto* Him whom he believed' (see
the margin of our Authorised Version), 'even God,
who calleth things which are not as though they
were,' prove that Abraham's faith was 'like' or
'answering to' (κατέναντι) that of the God in Whom
he trusted. The way, too, in which all through
Heb. xi. πίστει comes in in every case to show the
force or power by which all the wonders there recorded were accomplished, proves to me that the use
of this word in verse 3 must be in accordance with
all the rest, showing the power by which God worked
in the creation. I translate this 3rd verse of Heb. xi.
thus : 'By faith (so we understand) the worlds were
framed by the word of God,' &c. As to God's faith,
St. Mark xi. 22 has this very expression, calling on
us as sons of God to have the faith of God our
Father. Other passages of Holy Scripture teach the
same.

Would not your 'kind critic' allow that in the

Persons of the ever-blessed Trinity there must be faith or confidence in each other ? Could the Eternal Son really be Son, and yet not *trust* the Father ? Could the Father be the Father, and yet not *hope* in the Son ? Is God indeed love ? If so, can there be any love without faith or confidence in the beloved ? . . . How, if you read verse 3, 'Through faith we understand,' can our understanding through or by faith be the 'substance of things hoped for' ? But *God's creation by faith* is proof that 'faith is the substance of things hoped for.' . . . As to hope, it seems to me that such language as 'the God of hope' as much shows hope in God as the words 'the God of patience' and 'the God of all grace' prove that 'patience' and 'all grace' are in Him. . . . This I am sure of, that the life of hell is not only loveless but faithless and hopeless. Take faith and hope out of the life of heaven—say that love only is required there—do you not impoverish heaven ?

WOMEN'S DANGERS

As you most truly say, 'This is a dangerous time for women.' For powers of all kinds are pressing into the world, and the most sensitive natures are those which will be most sorely tried.

GOD'S CONSOLATION

The fact that God is love, and not a stoic, makes much possible in Him which at first we might perhaps suppose impossible. If He can be 'grieved,' why should we refuse Him παράκλησις also? especially when again and again He uses such words as, 'I found Israel like grapes in the wilderness; I saw your fathers as the first-ripe in the fig tree at her first time.'

THE SACRIFICIAL LIFE OF GOD

I go with every word you say of Sacrifice being inherent in God. I wanted to say something about it in my book on the 'Sacrifice of the New Man,' and indeed have just glanced at it (p. 180); but the subject is too deep except for a very few. But the mystery of the Eternal Generation of the ever-blessed Trinity contains it all; and so does the outgoing of the Word in nature. It is all sacrifice, if man could but see it. Christ only revealed God. He showed what is. His Incarnation is the great sacrament.

GOD A MOURNER

Your letter touches me, for the chord you strike of sorrow for loved ones lost or gone is one which

vibrates very loudly in me.   But I feel assured that
all is well—that ' blessed are the mourners '—because
sorrow is the very stuff that real joy is made of.
You will see it clearly some day.   I see it dimly even
now.   I see that love must suffer in this world ; yet
who would therefore wish to be without love?   God
is love : therefore He also suffers.   And God too has,
if I may say so, once lost His loved ones.   For man
is His dead son.   But He has found His lost, and
so shall we ; and because He has suffered through
the loss of His loved ones, He can feel for us who so
suffer.   Do you know that the Gospel actually puts
these words into the mouth of God, ' Rejoice with Me,
for this My son was dead and is alive again, he
was lost and is found ' ?   Oh, what comfort for
mourners !   Death is overcome in Christ.   By Christ's
death and resurrection God has got back His lost
ones ; and by the same death and resurrection we
shall surely find our own.

WHY A FALL WAS PERMITTED

Why any fall was permitted is a far deeper question.   It may suffice here to say that we must be
outside a thing to see it.   The valley sees the hill,
the hill the valley.   Without sin we should never
have fully known what our God is.   How could Christ

have shown His love and power if there had been no sickness to heal, no death to conquer?

SEERS

Real seers do often misinterpret their own true visions. Even the gift of tongues by the Holy Ghost requires an interpreter. . . . My own conviction is that all our first seeings always need to be corrected.

POETS

I am a great debtor to poems. Poets always seem to me to say deeper things than other teachers; perhaps deeper than they themselves are conscious of. For they speak out of the heart, and the heart is the real seer, often shaming the head, which thinks it knows so well.

CHRISTIAN EVIDENCE

To me the Gospel is its own witness. If I am in the sunshine, do I need proofs that the sun gives light and warmth? Here is a book which has fed and taught men as no other writing has ever done, which has been not a dead letter but a living friend to thousands. And some now profess to have discovered that it is all a pious fraud. Does a pious fraud feed souls and open eyes and give new life?

According to this theory we gather grapes of thorns and figs of thistles. There are still some who not only doubt the authenticity of the Gospel according to St. John, but who cannot believe that there ever was such a man as Jesus Christ, or at least that He was such as the Gospels describe Him. As for His resurrection, it is 'incredible.' And so-called believers are not a little to blame for the current unbelief. Christ is little known, or at least He is known rather as One who once was than as One who still is present with us. Is He, or is He not, really present with men, as in the days of His flesh? If He is, must there not be some other evidence accessible besides the historical? Does not the stress which is so generally laid on the outward or carnal evidence of the past prove that too many so-called believers have not yet attained to the knowledge of the spiritual evidences of the present? Those who doubt now would have doubted had they been on earth when the works were wrought which the Gospels tell of. All did not then believe. Why not? This is a great question.

' THE WORD OF THE LORD TRIED HIM '

I feel that the Lord Himself is coming out of His place, and that the veil which so long has hid Him

H

will be taken away, so that books like mine may not be needed. Still, there may be years and even generations before the final crisis comes, and during these years God may still use what He gives me to write. I feel that He gave it to me, and that it was His will that I should write it, and therefore I commit it to Him to do what He will with it. With any child of promise there must be special trials of faith. Others may be fruitful when they will. Abraham, Isaac, and Jacob, with the promise that their seed shall be as the stars of heaven, are one and all for long years barren ; and Joseph, with the vision of the sun and moon and stars bowing down before him, is himself long years in an Egyptian prison, where ' until the time that his word came ; the word of the Lord tried him.' Of course he had trials from men—to be rejected by his brethren, and to be forgotten by some whom he had comforted ; but the main temptation was not this, but rather that God's promise seemed to fail, though indeed it never failed and never could fail ; and so ' the word of the Lord tried him.' There is only one path for the elect. There can be no real rest here, save only in the living God our Saviour. The battle lasts to the very end of this pilgrimage, though spite of the outward battle there is also perfect peace. Do you remember, or did you ever see, the old lines—

Does the road wind up-hill all the way?
  Yes, to the very end.
Will the day's journey take the whole long day?
  From morn to night, my friend.

But every step of it is for us, and it is blessed that it is all 'uphill' and not downwards, ever upwards and onwards, till we come where Christ has gone before.

As to your dear husband, whom I constantly remember in my prayers, speaking after the manner of men, I can truly say that I grieve to hear of his continued suffering. . . .

May we not both—I mean your dear husband and myself—rejoice in this and in all things, that by all these things we are really being delivered from ourselves? Even our very failings are for us, for they make us despair of self, and fall as poor, empty, needy, helpless creatures into the loving arms of One who cannot fail us. Better, far better, to go hence with low thoughts of ourselves, however these may have been produced, than with the awful notion that we are 'not as other men.' It is the great saints that I tremble for, who have a character to keep up with men, and who are praised and flattered here by everybody. True saints have always been rejected. Look at the Lord—look at Paul and John, and the Apostles,

who were made as the filth of the earth and the off-
scouring of all things. But in their prisons or in
their Patmos heaven opened. When they were weak,
then were they strong.

MOTHERHOOD AND THE BLESSED VIRGIN

The mystery of the Holy Incarnation seems to you
to show some special relation which ordinary mothers,
far above fathers, hold to the children which are conceived or begotten naturally. To me, the miraculous
conception of our Lord speaks of another matter
altogether. To me, therefore, your assumption that
the Virgin Motherhood of Mary resembles ordinary
motherhood, or can teach any special lesson respecting
it, is a mistake. Motherhood of Christ is only granted
to a Virgin. And the relation of the Virgin to her
Son is the relation not of ordinary mothers to their
children, but of the virgin-affection in every soul,
whether in man or woman, which receives the Word
of God, to the New Man, or Christ, which is conceived
or brought forth in us. . . . Surely, outward and
earthly motherhood has enough to stand on in its
special powers over those it bears, without assuming
that the peculiar prerogatives of the miraculous and
Virgin Motherhood of Christ are the distinctive lot

and right of all mothers.   Unless I greatly err, the
two motherhoods are most distinct and different.

1883

BODILY HEALINGS

Your question as to bodily healings by faith is an
interesting one.   The subject for many years has
been before my thoughts.   I have not a doubt as to
the power of faith, now as ever, to obtain and work
not healings of the body only, but almost all sorts of
earthly deliverance.   It must be so, for God is the
same unchanging God, and ' all things are possible to
him that believeth.'   We have, too, so many authenticated cases of healing, not only in our own day, and
from men of all creeds, but also in the centuries since
the Apostles' days, that I do not see how we can refuse
to acknowledge them.   Almost everything except
death is said to have been cured by some believer.   I
do not know that since the Apostles' days there is an
authenticated instance of a dead man being raised up
again to live this present dying life, though there are
many such cases in the old Jewish dispensation.   But
while I believe that there have been and yet are
healings wrought by faith—physical or bodily healings,

I mean, for there can be question about the spiritual—
I greatly doubt whether such bodily healings properly
belong to this present dispensation. I see from 1 Cor.
xii. 28 and James v. 15 that such healings were
acknowledged in the transitional period from the
Jewish to the Christian dispensations. They seem to
me to belong rather to that which was in the flesh.
For we, as Christians, start from baptism, which is
death to present nature, and not any saving or improvement of it; though we look for a new and
spiritual body, a house not made with hands, and
indeed 'have' (as St. Paul says, 2 Cor. v. 1) the
beginnings of it already in the new man, . . . that
new man, though unseen, being even now 'created in
righteousness and true holiness.' I know many
believers still live after the flesh, and hate the Cross,
and strive to make themselves as comfortable as they
can on earth, and shrink from anything and everything that involves a daily death. But this shrinking
does not prove that this living after the flesh is
according to the mind of this dispensation. Of
course, faith upon any platform will always get what
it seeks from God ; and many truly believing souls
are yet practically, that is, as far as their experience
goes, only in the 'Jews' religion,' still 'through fear
of death subject to bondage ; ' and God being ever

unchanging, must necessarily meet their prayer and
faith as He met those of David and Hezekiah. But
such faith may be rather Jewish than Christian faith.
Even in Christian faith, 'faith *in* Christ' is one
thing, while 'the faith *of* Christ' is quite another.
You have, of course, noticed how St. Paul speaks of 'the
faith of Christ,' which we are called to have, as well
as the 'faith in Christ,' which draws all blessings from
Him. Faith in Christ was shown by the leper, and
the woman of Canaan, and others, who were healed
by Christ while He was in the flesh ; and a like faith
is yet shown *in* Him by those who seek a blessing
from Him. But this faith in Him is very different
from the 'faith *of* Christ' which we are called to have,
and which, even in the presence of death and darkness,
though it could call for twelve legions of angels and
get them, yet only says, 'If it be possible, let this cup
pass from Me : nevertheless, not My will, but Thine, be
done.' The eleventh chapter of Hebrews also shows
that there is a faith which obtains promises, and
another, perhaps a greater, which 'received not the
promises.' It seems to me that the healings of the
Gospel wrought on men's bodies, at the end of and
during the continuance of the carnal dispensation,
are the external witnesses of the spiritual healings
which Christ is working daily, and will work to the

end by His members, to meet men's real sickness. I
see that to this day lepers are cleansed, the dead are
raised, the storms are stilled, bread is increased ; but
the works are wrought not in the flesh, but in the
spirit ; for, as I have said, we are come, or should be
come, out of the carnal dispensation into a spiritual
one, the body being now dead by the Cross of Christ,
and to be reckoned dead by us, while a new man is
formed or being formed in us.   But cannot God
change these 'vile bodies' by His Spirit, and make
them conquerors over death as well as over sickness ?
Surely He can and will.   But when this is really done,
it will not be the ' vile body ' kept from sickness by
faith, but a transformation of the whole man, making
us, like Christ, conquerors over death and hell for ever.

TRUTH AND LOVE

The peril . . . is that souls are tempted and
caught, not by a lie, but by a truth.   Truth is the
bait.   As I said to your dear people, if you want to
catch birds, you spread some good seed near the trap
—husks will not catch them ; and if you can only
get some sweet-singing bird, who is already caught,
to act as a decoy, so much the better for the bird-
catcher, so much the worse for the poor birds. . . .

A zealous young convert, full of zeal, with little knowledge of the bitter fruits of sectarianism, is used even through the very Gospel he preaches sometimes to pull souls into some trap of sectarianism. What is the remedy? Love first, love second, love third. Live and die for the dear souls, even as Christ did. Love must conquer, for God is love.

WORKING AND WAITING

One of the commonest temptations of this and of every age is to rush into work before we are distinctly called to and fitted for it. God's work needs preparation. Think of the years of unnoticed toil at Nazareth in the case of our Blessed Lord, and the years, too, in Arabia with the Apostle Paul. Of course, if you have a distinct call from the Lord, and plainly see that it is a call, your duty and privilege is at once to answer it. But he that believeth will not make haste. The Lord may call you suddenly, but that which comes suddenly from the Lord is always gradually prepared for. Meanwhile and always walk in love and grace to all.

THE SPIRIT AND OUTWARD FORMS

The subject of your letter is an important one, and one, as the Quakers and so-called Brethren have

shown us, on which it is easy to err on the right hand
as much as on the left.   In the narrow way of the
true life we must 'turn neither to the right hand nor
to the left.'   The truth, or 'right hand,' which the
old Quakers and so-called Brethren rightly pressed,
was, that the Spirit of God was needed by the Church,
and that without the Spirit all our labours would be
more or less fruitless.   The error, or 'left hand,' into
which they wandered is manifold, arising mainly
from their practical, though unintentional, denial of
the Incarnation, and from their looking for a vague
spirit in their assemblies to guide them, instead of a
Christed, that is, an anointed, Man.   God's way of
salvation is by a Man, and men who are Christ's
members, who are indeed anointed with the Holy
Ghost and power, but who act as men, and not as a
vague influence, in guiding and feeding the Church.
Thus, when St. Paul speaks of the gifts of the Spirit,
he does not say, 'He gave some apostleship, and
some prophecy, and some pastorship, and some teaching;' but rather, 'He gave some apostles, and some
prophets, and some evangelists, and some pastors and
teachers;' for the gifts of the Spirit were men, even
as Christ is a man.   Therefore the Corinthians,
though they had all sorts of spiritual powers among
them—'every one with a psalm, or a doctrine, or a

tongue, or a revelation, or an interpretation '—needed
a man like Paul, who was anointed with the Spirit,
to direct and keep them in order, saying that the
meetings were to be arranged thus or thus, and ending with the words, 'Let all things be done decently
and *in order* ;' which last words are literally,
'according to arrangement.' And all this, because in
Christ man is one with God for ever, at His right
hand, far above all principalities and powers. But
this is what both the Quakers and the Plymouth
Brethren object to. 'Nothing is to be arranged,'
they say, 'all is to be left to the guidance of the
Spirit at the time.' If they were only consistent—
—but happily they are not—they would never fix the
hour for the Lord's Supper, or indeed for any meeting. It would be 'left open,' as they are so fond of
saying ; which practically means that disorder is
better than order, and that the most forward person
may talk and do just what he likes. Of course I
believe that, in a carnal dispensation and among
carnal people, the Spirit may at times come suddenly
on certain people, as on Samson and Jephthah, leading
them to do this or that at some special juncture, and
that God may yet so work with carnal souls. But if
we are really 'Christed,' or anointed, the Spirit
abides ; and a truly Christed man is, after that

anointing, always able to speak, and always able also
(which may be harder) to hold his tongue.

One special mistake both of the Quakers and of
Plymouth Brethren is the notion that a form hinders
the Spirit. Nothing can be a greater delusion. The
Spirit, like air or water, can fill any form, if only it
is received. You may, indeed, have bottles without
wine ; but if you wish to keep the wine the bottles
are useful. It is the miserable fact that so many
professed believers and ministers are 'bottles without
wine' which makes these Plymouth people cry out so
much against bottles. But bottles have their use.
All forms are bottles. Life always makes itself a
form to dwell in. The body without the spirit is
dead, but the spirit without the body is vagabond.
Christ and His Apostles are the pattern—the Spirit
in a man, that is, in a form—not the Spirit without
a form. And the fact that so much of Holy Scripture
is written acrostically, that is, according to the letters
of the alphabet, shows that the Holy Spirit is not
hindered by a form, but can fill any, as air fills any
vessel. . . . The Spirit of God is not weaker than
the spirit of the world. The spirit of the world, the
spirit of self, can get into any form, even God's form
—into prayer, into fasting, into almsgiving. Cannot
the Spirit of God, the Spirit of Love, fill the forms of

this world? The Incarnation is the answer. God's fullness dwells in a man, that it may dwell in us. The Quakers were consistent in rejecting forms. They would have no Bibles or hymn-books. The Spirit was to be all and to do all. See the retribution for practically denying the Incarnation. Their hat is a form, their coat is a form, their tongue, with its 'thee' and 'thou,' is a form. The Plymouth Brethren, happily for them, are inconsistent, but they too are receiving their retribution in the spirit which is among them causing endless splits and quarrels. The sad fact is that neither Quakers nor Plymouth Brethren understand the Incarnation. I speak, of course, of their system. Some individuals among them may see more, or at least be prevented from gross mistakes, through what by grace they learnt before they became Plymouth Brethren. But in each of these bodies, Quakers and Plymouth Brethren, the sacraments, which are extensions of the Incarnation, are undervalued. It must be so. Comparative anatomy is a real science. From one limb you can make out the whole body. Both these systems look rather for some vague influence than for a present Christ, an Anointed Man, who lives and works and helps us by His flesh, and by His Spirit in His members. The fact is that, wherever and whenever God works, He works by a man, or by men, that is, by a form, whether in Gospel preaching or in instructing believers. And the reason is, because God's method is the Incarnation.

WE NEED ALL THINGS

How we learn by all these things that really we need all—that there is no one whom we can do without, for indeed Christ needs (if we may say so), and will surely one day possess, all. I know how at an early stage of our heavenward journey we seem to think that we can get there, if not alone, yet without a vast multitude of those who have been bought by the precious blood of Christ, and whom surely He loves, for He is love. I know how, in the same imperfect and partial spirit, there are many things in ourselves which we would destroy, simply because as yet, through our weakness, we cannot rule them. I think I begin to see how everything is needed, and all are needed. The very flesh, which so grieves us, is, to use the old alchemical formula, something of a solvent, and helps to melt the hardness of the poor captive soul, who even by the very badness (as we say) and weakness of its environs, while here, learns something of its own imperfections. The old alchemists used to say that in the perfect transformation and transmutation, accomplished by the stone, nothing could be thrown away without some loss, and that every portion even of what seemed dross was needed for bringing about the glorious end, when the dark earthly creature should be transfigured into transparent gold.   If I do not see this fully, I at least begin to see it.   We need everything and all.   God has made no mistakes, even though through our blindness we think some things are simply horrible. They are horrible, if they were the end.   But they are only the stages to the end.   So for all things, for pictures, which some despise, and for music, and for dress, and for things far lower than these, which, even to a converted soul, seem at first unnecessary, let us bless and thank our blessed God.   All things are ours, even if, as children, we cannot use them.

CHRISTMAS

Christ is the witness and sacrament of God's will and purpose touching men, even to dwell in man in all His fullness, to make man His heir, by man to overcome all evil and sickness and sorrow, by man to cast out devils, by man to break the gates of death and hell.   It has all been wrought for us in One Man, Christ Jesus.   God's will is that it shall be wrought in man, and first in those who by grace are first-fruits.

Why do we not even now know more of this eternal
life? Only because we do not enough accept the
humiliation and the cross, which is the way to it,
through the waters and the fires to the right hand of
God.

MISUNDERSTANDINGS

You are 'not understood' as you would be. Is
God understood? Was the Perfect Lord understood,
even by His disciples? Did His words never 'scare'
any? Was it 'wounded self-love' in Him which made
Him groan? Do not judge yourself or your work too
hardly. 'Judge not' applies to self-judgment with
tender souls.

HIGH CHURCHMEN

I thought you . . . would be interested in J.'s
letter. It is one of the thousand proofs which I have
had of the very true and simple faith which there
is in some of the young so-called Ritualists. Being
such a one as I am, who can find work anywhere,
while as yet I have had no place of my own on earth
where I can lay my spirit's head, I have, by God's
providence, been led to see, what so few see, . . .
how true and simple, and how really alike also, is the
faith and love which exists in schools of thought

apparently the most opposite. In High Church and
in Low Church I see the same one light of God—
in one the red, in another the yellow, in a third the
blue ray. Very few have all the rays united in the
one white light; yet all are lovely in their working.
C. at the East End, with his rough Protestant Evangelicalism, is beautiful in his place. The red ray is
very strong in him. The Broad Churchman, too, has
his beauty. And to me the High Churchman, if true,
is no less beautiful. I see in the last, I mean in the
High Churchman, the beauty of having a mother,
or rather, of having a very devoted appreciation of a
mother's claims and of her value. 'Mother Church'
is always in their mouths and in their hearts. For
they feel they owe her not a little. Of course there
is an evil in boys having been brought up only by a
mother, good as she may be. But children brought
up without the training of a mother lose immensely.
I think I see this with those who think little of
Mother Church, because they have never known her.
As a result they are brought up by the servants and
catch their vulgarities, and very rarely have their
self-will broken. They may gain independence, like
boys cast on the world without a mother : they lose
manners. Dear J. is one who shows in every word
that he has been brought up near his mother.

I

Surely there are perils on this side also. The child may be spoilt, or the mother may be fallen and unfaithful; yet it is always beautiful to me to see this reverence for the mother.

SYMPATHY OF HEARERS

Well do I remember that meeting, and dear Mrs. B.'s eagerness to draw all sorts of things from me. Such hearers are like magnets. . . . At least, they always act on me; for my addresses depend much on my audience. Some shut me quite up, and some open my heart. Women as a rule are receptive, and therefore help a speaker. They 'assist,' not only in the French sense of the word, but in our more practical interpretation of it.

MARRIAGE WITH WIFE'S SISTER

It is indeed cause for thankfulness that the abominable Bill as to marriage with sisters is again rejected. I could not but exclaim from my heart and with my voice, as soon as I opened the paper this morning, 'Thank God!'

TRAVEL IN THE HOLY LAND

What A. K. says of the relative and comparative influence of imaginative and so-called strong practical natures struck me as being singularly correct—that imaginative people, however able, are weak in forcing their will on others, being influencers rather than repressors ; and yet that these imaginative sympathetic souls do *alter* those with whom they live, by persuading them by their influence, even more than those apparently, and perhaps really, stronger natures, who *subdue* others by their strong will. All that A. K. says, too, of the distastefulness of those who bear their brethren's burdens to those who are always judging everything, though it is the common experience of the saints, is rarely put so well and clearly. . . .

But all this must be somewhat alien to your thoughts on first entering Jerusalem ; though indeed the Blessed One, Whom above all others we cannot help remembering in Jerusalem, was marked by these two characteristics as much as any, first—that He was an influence rather than a repressor, and altered those around Him not so much by forcibly subduing as by permeating them by His holy quiet influence ; and secondly, that His not judging, but rather bearing with, the faults of others was one of His greatest offences in the eyes of the self-made saints of His day, for which they upbraided Him in the well-known words, ' This man receiveth sinners and eateth with them.' How you will delight to trace His steps ! And

of some spots there can be no doubt. . . . I shall
never forget those days I spent going round Jerusalem,
especially when I could be alone for a while in some
place where I knew the Lord had been. The Egyptian
temples magnetised me : I mean, they seemed sometimes, as I sat among their ruined columns, to be
alive again almost with the kings and priests and
slaves who once thronged them. I shall never forget
how the nearly choked-up passage in the temple at
Eleusis affected me in the same manner, when I
remembered that every Greek of note, whose names
I had repeated from my childhood, had there been
initiated into the so-called 'lesser mysteries,' that is,
some of the first-learnt secrets, as far as the Greeks
understood them, of this wonderful riddle of our
present life and death. But no place, I think, so
touched me as some of the scenes in and around
Jerusalem. And the tears of some poor Russian
peasants, who had come as pilgrims from (I think)
near Moscow, and who were kissing every stone of the
little path up the Mount of Olives, by the side of the
Garden of Gethsemane, seemed to call out fresh
sympathy in me. To them it was all so real—Christ
had so really been there—that their faith and love
stimulated mine. And when I thought what it must
have cost them to get there, and how poor and suffer-

ing some of them looked—women, who had certainly
walked every step from Jaffa—I could not rest till
I had shared my lunch with them. How on such
journeys, and indeed all through life, one meets souls
for a moment whom we may never see again, but yet
are linked to one in Christ, and, though in very
different ways to ours, yet trust and love Him.

1884

MATTER AND SPIRIT: THE GNOSTICS

The question of the use of so-called 'matter' for
the redemption of fallen 'spirit' is a deep one. There
most be a loving and wise reason for all that is or
exists ; and certainly the trials and sorrows of this
outward life are used of God for the perfecting and
cleansing of the fallen soul or spirit. It is wonderful
what glimpses or gleams of light there are, mixed
with error doubtless, in some of the views or speculations of the early Gnostics. I have lately been
going through Hippolytus again, and find that there
is nothing new. Almost every speculation of later
days has been anticipated by some one or other of
the Gnostic schools. I was greatly interested among
other things to see how some of the Gnostic sects

used up all or a great part of the Greek mythology
as an imperfect prefiguring of the Lord. Among
other things, connected with the spiritual sense of the
story of Proserpine and Ceres (to which I have
alluded in my 'New Man'), I see that Hippolytus
dwells on the mystical name of the place where
these mysteries were celebrated, namely, Eleusis, or
'Coming,' for the mystery of birth, and of the new
birth from the grave, is a 'coming.' What wonders
there are everywhere, if we could only see them!

ST. ANDREW'S DAY

Last night's post brought me your very welcome
letter, . . . timed so exactly to reach me on the Eve
or Vigil of St. Andrew's. Would that I had some
greater claim than your loving imagination to link
me with that first Apostle, whom I have often longed
to be conformed to, but to whom I have as yet had
very little resemblance, save perhaps in this, that I
have borne his name, and have wished also both in
life and death to be more like him. I well remember,
at Patras, looking at the exact spot which tradition
yet points out as the place, just facing the heathen
temple of Ceres, where for two long days and nights,
after a week of imprisonment and severe scourging,
the true St. Andrew hung lingeringly, tied with cords

to a cross, to die there of exhaustion. And I saw
there, what you too, I think, have seen, how not a
little of that old heathen temple is now built in as
a part of the cathedral of St. Andrew, which for
centuries has stood close to the spot where the poor
mocked disciple breathed his last as a bound malefactor. I wish nothing better myself than to be like
him; and not least in this, that, though the first of all to
follow Christ, he was content to be not first in honour,
but to be placed lower than his brother, anywhere the
Blessed Lord was pleased to place him. Certainly
the words to him and to his brother, 'Follow Me, and
I will make you,' have for I know not how many years
been a sort of sentence for me. And, wretchedly as
I have followed, even in my poor following I have
been '*made*' and '*made by Christ*,' and have
seen and found things which have given me more
delight and deeper glimpses of wisdom and beauty
than all the sights of Italy and Greece, though
these too have delighted me. I feel sure that what
the Lord can 'make' us if we 'follow' Him is more
than all the world can make us. I think too that
seeing what the Lord opens if we 'follow' Him,
though in one way it spoils us for looking at the
world, yet also surely opens to us a depth of meaning
in all things here, which we shall never see until the

Lord has opened something of the so-called unseen
world to us.   I know that my dear old friend and
fellow-traveller . . . who in bygone years went with
me through not a little of the beautiful land where
you are now sojourning, used again and again to say
of me that I was 'the worst sight-seer he had ever
travelled with ; ' while I yet believe that I saw some
things which he never saw.   For instead of rushing
from sight to sight, really seeing nothing, it pleased
me more to contemplate a single face or picture,
perhaps of Raphael's or Giotto's, which thus became
to me, as I think it was to the painter, a sort of
shadow of something far fairer than even the lovely
thing it represented.

BAPTISM: MAURICE AND PUSEY

I have a very vivid recollection of [the controversy
between Maurice and Pusey as to baptism], for what
both those beloved men wrote upon the subject helped
me, brought up as I had been in a very different
school, to whom baptism was almost nothing.   Pusey's
words as to what we receive of life through Christ,
I shall never forget.   Both my first little books, that
on the ' Offerings ' and also that on ' The Differences of
the Four Gospels,' quote a long passage from Pusey's
Tract on Baptism, which I shall remember as long as

I live, showing how really we receive eternal life through our Lord Jesus Christ. After this, and not long after, Maurice helped me in another way, by leading me to see that God's relation to man, which the Incarnation witnessed to, was the revelation of an existing fact, and that baptism was the continual and abiding witness of the fact of this relationship. The first of these beloved men pressed that the Incarnation is the *means* by which we receive the life : the other, that the same Incarnation is the *pledge* and sign which assures us of it. Both were right in what they affirmed.

PERFECTION

The way of our perfecting is not at all as we think it will be. Christ in His own perfecting was troubled, and much more have His dearest children, when they can bear it, to know something, however little, of the same experience. . . . The first walk with Christ, when we are just emerging from being disciples of some burning and shining light like John the Baptist, who has said to us, ' Behold the Lamb of God,' and when we say to Jesus, ' Master, where dwellest Thou ? ' and He answers, ' Come and see,' and we come and see and abide with Him for a season, is to our poor thoughts a far more blessed walk than that of the two disciples, some years later, when 'their eyes were holden that they should not know Him,' and when He said, 'What manner of communications are these that ye have one to another as ye walk and are sad?' Yet the latter walk is a long way in advance of the first, though to flesh and blood far more sorrowful. It was the beginning of their real understanding of the Cross, and the way to their knowledge of the resurrection.   It is hard to explain these things. Experience only really explains them.   Yet one to whom the way is familiar may say to another, Be of good cheer under the trial—it is the appointed way for all who have really desired to be conformed to Christ.   I am sure of this.   For it is thus that the selfhood dies.   And till it dies we are not perfected. Of course, even from the first, we all of us understand something of the movements or working of self in the sensual or social spheres of life ; but who at first is aware of the immense strength and subtlety of this same self in all of us in what we count religion, when, as is the case in our earlier days, we throw our whole will into the discharge of religious duties, and make great progress in the religious life, and seem to our-selves and others to be growing rapidly in heavenly gifts ; and yet all this may be the life of truth if not from self yet still in self ; and the utter privation of such a life is not the extinction of truth and love, but rather, though at the time we do not understand it, its vivification.

DEPRESSION

I am so thankful to hear that, through the Lord's mercy, the depression of spirits which burdened you has passed away. I feel sure that, trying as it was, that very depression was all for you and not against you—that we are never safer than when we are depressed and burdened, even as we are never in greater peril than when our cup of joy, whether temporal or spiritual, is overflowing. Yet we naturally long for more than safety, even for comfort; and the Lord gives it us when we can bear it.

1885

BODILY HEALINGS

You seem to think that I possess a power which I am unwilling to exercise on your behalf. It is not so. If I could heal you, I would. But the gift which Christ exercises through me lies more in healing spiritual diseases . . . than in restoring sick bodies. And my conviction is that, with truly converted souls,

healing of the body is not always granted, because
pain and sickness may be doing for our soul's eternal
good far more than health of body can do. Would
sickness be allowed, if it were not to fulfil some
gracious end? I feel assured that by sickness souls
are taught more than by health.

You say that your 'health and sight are matters
of the greatest importance to you,' and hint that the
state of your eyes may possibly hinder your professional
career. This is surely a great trial for you. And,
in my judgment, you are entirely justified in seeking
and using every lawful means for your restoration.
But, after all, there is something more important than
our work or living in this world. And the trial
which lies upon you may be the very cross which is
sent to perfect you. It cannot be in vain that in Holy
Scripture we have so many exhortations to patience,
and to ' count it all joy when we fall into divers trials
or temptations.' If we are ever to be conformed to
Christ, it can only be through trials, in which we learn
to say, ' Thy will be done.'

Do I then advise you to do nothing, or do I blame
you for using all probable means, whether spiritual or
physical, for your recovery? Not at all. I think it
one of the mistakes of our Faith-healing brethren that
they blame souls for using all the ordinary means at

their disposal. God is a God of means. Christ Himself is a means, and Himself used means, as in the clay and saliva, and in the pool of Siloam, and the priests to whom He sent some. Food and clothing are means of health, which we are bound to use; so, in my view, is medicine and the skill of the physician. These are all God's gifts to do us good. You are therefore, I think, quite right in using such or any other like means. Only, use them as God's gifts, not as in His place, but as His ministrations to you. Use the faith of brethren, too, if they have faith. Then leave all to God. If your body is not then healed, there must be some loving reason for it. If you wish to come here, I will specially pray with you and for you. But I can do nothing without Christ. And Christ is with you and in you where you are. He could of old heal by a word and at a distance as well as by a touch. He can still through me or without me heal by His word, which is in you and with you. Will you sit quite quiet and think of Him in you and with you, your very life? Will you, in entire submission to His will, lay your burden fully before Him? Tell Him everything—how you wish for health, that you may continue in your profession and support those whom He has given you. Tell Him that you are sure He can help you if He will, and that if the

sickness comes as a chastening for any known or
unknown sin, you ask His pardon and deliverance.
And then leave all with Him. If you are still left
to suffer, be sure it is for your eternal good.

MALE AND FEMALE

Thank you for Mrs. Oliphant's book. . . . If I
understand it, its purpose is to teach that the advance
or perfecting of our nature is by union with and
reception of the creaturely spirits which are around
us, whose union with us is to complete what is lacking
in our present divided state.   Is this the teaching of
the Gospel of Christ, or is it not rather a going back
to that of which all heathen antiquity is so full, and
which Christianity when it was very full of life swept
away for a season—namely, the seeking to creaturely
spirits within the veil, rather than waiting to be filled
with the Creator Spirit?   If I understand the Gospel,
its teaching is that man is perfected by union with
God.   Christ is the model of men's perfect restoration.
Was He perfected by creaturely spirits as counter-
parts, or by God's indwelling Spirit?   If He is the
' Way,' then the right path seems to me that the Word
of God should come into our divided nature to bring
into it the seed of the true and perfect humanity, that
is, the seed of a Divine Nature ; and that then, by

death to present nature, that is, by the Cross and by a resurrection from the dead, the fallen and divided creature should be brought out of its division into the full enjoyment of its true and real being. The question really is, Was Christ made perfect? Was He, as man, 'made perfect through sufferings,' as the Gospel teaches, or by some creaturely spirits uniting themselves to Him to enlighten His darkness and to give Him power? Did He come to highest heaven by any creaturely counterpart, or by the Creator Spirit? The Gospel answers, He was anointed by the Holy Ghost, and then, as man, brought by the Cross out of the divided life to man's true place of perfect union with God. Is there now any more perfect way than this old way of the new birth, and Cross, and resurrection?

Of course, in any testimony to catch souls in these last days there must be some, and perhaps much, precious truth. Some forgotten truth, which the carnal Church has lost sight of, would of course be attractive. The truth of God's and of man's duality is such a truth, familiar to the saints, though few now understand it. So is the truth of man's having been clothed with a fleshly beastlike body when he was turned out of Paradise, the 'coats of skins.' So, of course, is the great truth that Two are One in a Third in God. All this you will find in St. Ambrose

and St. Augustine. But the old Church held that a
mixture of creaturely seeds, the 'sons of God' with
the 'daughters of men,' brought on the Flood, the
saved family being marked by separation from such
a mixture. I cannot go into all this now. Of course
spirits are pressing into the world, for the Lord is
coming. Many of the spirits, as it seems to me, are
weak, false, and evil. But holy angels are always
ministering to us. Thank God, too, the Blessed Spirit
of God is also calling us to conformity with the life and
death of Christ. Are we not 'complete in Him'?

THE HISTORIC CHRIST

Some of the members of the Hermetic Society, you
tell me, object to or deny the 'outward or historic
Christ.' These objectors wish, I suppose, to be philo-
sophical; but are these denials philosophy? For is
there or is there not such a thing as the flesh or outward body? If it is all Maya, or illusion, what do these
objectors object to? If, speaking after the manner of
men, there is such a thing as flesh, what are its relations
to man, and what are its destinies? The Gospel says
that this outward body is of the earth earthy; the
present seen world being a creation out of the *débris*
of a former spiritual outbirth; and that Christ came
into it to redeem it, as well as the man who is now cap-

tive in it : this redemption of the fallen nature in the Person of Jesus of Nazareth being the pledge that all outward nature and creature, which yet groans in travail, shall, because God has come into it and is in it, be delivered. Is there not an outward world : an outer as well as an inner court ? If so, what is to be its end ? The Gospel of Christ, that is, Christ Himself, says that it is all to be transmuted—to ' perish and be changed '—wonderful and blessed words, and that this work has already been done in a part of the fallen creation, in the ' first-fruits,' even in the flesh of Christ, which was and is the witness that God will dwell in the creature, even in its present divided state, through death to bring it back to dwell in Him, of twain thus making one again for ever. All this has been done in the flesh or Incarnation of the Lord. He is the sacrament of our redemption ; and, as a sacrament, is Himself the union of the Word of God with flesh or a creature form, which henceforth becomes, as the Church teaches, ' a means whereby we receive the same, and a pledge to assure us thereof.' The old Greek students of the Hermetic Mystery saw something at least of this ; as we see not only in the myth of Ceres and Proserpine, but in the direct witness and warning that, though at first we think it would be well wholly to be quit of flesh and blood, yet these are

K

needed, if only as a solvent; and that all, even that
which is most outward and carnal in us, has its
place and use, and can and will one day be transmuted perfectly. At all events, the Gospel teaches
that, whatever this outward nature is, Christ was.
If nature is ' historic,' then Christ is ' historic.' The
Word, which at creation was made nature, and
which was then made letter in the written law, was
made flesh in Jesus of Nazareth. For He came into
the outbirth to go through its necessary dissolution,
and bring it back through dissolution to its true and
real being. To say that, because every recorded fact
in the history of Christ is typical of the progress of
the regenerate soul, therefore that history was never
enacted in the plane of the seen creation, is as wise, or
as foolish, as to say that, because all visible creation
is a parable, therefore it is not outward or physical.
Surely, all nature, in seed-time and harvest, and
birth and death, and darkness and light, and indeed
in everything, is preaching the selfsame story as
Christ's life and death and resurrection. It is the
same tune, now sung in chorus, now in solo, now
played upon a larger, now upon a smaller instru-
ment. I do not touch the question whether man
is the greatest or the least. He is certainly the
epitome and hieroglyphic of the universe, with all

worlds or kingdoms in him. And in the literal outward Man, Jesus of Nazareth, born of a woman, the whole story of the way in which divided nature is to be brought back again into God is told out and shown before our eyes sacramentally. These objectors to the 'historic Christ' are Quakers in another form. They object to sacraments, or outward and visible signs of the inward and spiritual grace given to us. Well, only give them time and rope enough, and they will be punished, or punish themselves, exactly as the Quakers are, by becoming slaves to some other form, which is not of God's but of their own making, some *idolon specus*, if not *idolon fori*. . . . The history of the early Gnostics, who objected to an outward and historic Christ, professing to be seeking what was more spiritual, shows what such spirituality is worth. I say nothing of the shameless immorality which some of them at last openly professed. I only ask, Whom did they help? Did they ever reach or save sinners? It seems to me that nothing is so spiritual as true love, which can stoop to every form, even to coming in the flesh as God has done, even to the form of the slave and captive, to change it back into the lord and freeman.

EVANGELICALISM

The question of the truth or error of so-called 'Evangelicalism' . . . is too wide for such a letter as I can now write to you; nor do I much care to write on what appear to me to be simply imperfect views of doctrine; because in our Christian course we must all at first be wrong in many things, and because such mistakes, in my judgment, do not really hurt souls if they are meek and loving. What seems to me the real evil in this matter lies not so much in the error of certain views as in the self-conceit of those who hold them as their party-badge, and as the truth of God, which makes them, as they think, the special guardians of the Gospel. For you proclaim yourselves to be 'Evangelical,' and do not scruple to say of others that they 'do not preach the Gospel,' simply because their views of the sacraments and the Atonement differ more or less from yours. . . .

First . . . it seems to me that one great mistake of so-called Evangelicals lies in their practically making consciousness rather than fact the basis of what they call religion. Of course, in a large party there are shades of difference, and all good men are always better than their system; but with Evangelical people so called their state towards God is generally

measured by their sense or feeling of their state,
rather than by the fact and faith of what has been
done for them by the Incarnation, death, and resurrection of our Lord Jesus Christ. They are not children
of God (so they generally teach) until they feel or
know it, and can cry or say, 'Abba, Father.' They
are not, according to their Gospel, forgiven till they
feel and know that they are forgiven. As a rule, they
think they can tell exactly when the life of God began
in them. That time was when they felt their sins
were forgiven them. Consciousness or feeling is the
test. Strange to say, and yet not strange, none louder
than these men in teaching that by Adam's sin we
are all fallen and utterly condemned and dead in sins,
whether we are or are not conscious of it : Adam's sin
has ruined us apart from any act of ours, or any
consciousness of our death and ruin in and through
him. But Christ's work, so you teach, has not done
as much for us in the way of our restoration : till we
are conscious of our regeneration, that is, till our
conversion, we are not regenerate ; though St. Peter
distinctly says that we are 'begotten again to a lively
hope by the resurrection of Jesus Christ from the
dead.' I think that naturally we are all too prone to
make our feelings, rather than Christ's work and faith
in it, the test and measure of our standing before

God. Yet it seems to me that the so-called Evangelical system encourages and nourishes this tendency. . . . The two other great doctrinal mistakes of the so-called Evangelical party, as it seems to me, are their views of the sacraments or the Incarnation, and of the Atonement. As a rule, they undervalue, or at least think lightly, of all sacraments, not seeing that the Incarnation itself is a sacrament. . . . So, as to the Atonement. Their doctrine of substitution generally is that our Lord suffered that we should not suffer—that He died that we should not die. Some have gone so far in their explanation of vicariousness as to say that 'any act of our Lord's in which we can follow Him is not vicarious.' The logical conclusion from this statement would be, either that His death was not vicarious, or that we do not die. Some see this, and distinctly say (it has been said to me), that we do not die, and that, since Christ died for us, our death really is not death nor sin's penalty.

PSALM CXVIII

The 118th Psalm, the great concluding Passover hymn, which our Lord and His disciples sang just when He went out to be betrayed and crucified, tells the whole story—not only that we must be 'compassed about' with cares or cursing like 'bees,' while there is one who 'thrusts sore at us that we may fall,' but that 'the Lord Himself also chastens us sore.' And yet that of all this, if only our eyes are open, we can say, 'This is the gate of the Lord,' and 'This is the day that the Lord hath made.' There is no other gate or entrance into the spiritual life. 'Therefore we will rejoice and be glad in it.' This very day of trial is of the Lord. It is not the devil's doing. It is 'the day which the Lord hath made.' Dear W. will some day understand this psalm. How many years it took me to understand it, and really to say, 'Bind the sacrifice with cords.' 'Blessed is he, or blessed is that, which cometh in the Name of the Lord.' . . . It is the angel with the plagues which says, 'Come, I will show thee the Lamb's wife.'

1 COR. I. 21

The words are generally said to mean that 'after that, *in the wise purpose of God*, the world, *by its wisdom*, knew not God, it pleased God by the foolishness of preaching to save them that believe.' According to this interpretation, the same word, 'wisdom,' in the same sentence is made first to mean the wise purpose of God, and then to mean man's wisdom. But the wisdom which St. Paul speaks of is in both cases the same wisdom. The true sense is

this : ' After that, in the book of God's wisdom (which
men now call nature), the world, by and in all this
display of wisdom, failed (in consequence of its blindness) to know God, it pleased God by the foolishness
of preaching (that is, by speaking about Himself) to
save them that believe.' ' You cannot learn by My book
of wisdom,' says God, ' or by My works, which show
what I am on every side. Then I will teach you by
talking about Myself, which is foolishness.' ' Preaching ' is called ' the foolishness of God,' because in it
God speaks about Himself. The Gospel, or New
Covenant, is all, ' I will, I will, I will ; ' or to better
instructed souls, ' I am, I am, I am.' It is not
enough for fallen man to have on every side in the
works of God, that is, in His formed word, witness of
what God is, and that He can, and will, and does
bring life out of apparent death, and flowers and
sweetness out of dunghills, and colours out of soot,
and running water out of hard hailstones, and light
from buried coal, and diamonds out of charcoal, and
rubies out of mud ; and that He opens His hand and
satisfies the desire of every living thing. Men are so
utterly blind and dead to all that the formed word
teaches as to God's love and wisdom and care for His
creatures, that, to make us know Him, He is obliged
actually to talk about Himself, and to tell us that He

loves us and will have mercy upon us. And this speaking about Himself, as St. Paul says to the Corinthians, is 'speaking as a fool.' It is like a gentleman, whose behaviour as a gentleman goes for nothing among ignorant villagers, being obliged to say, ' I am a gentleman—I will really deal justly with you ; ' or like a father, spite of ceaseless kindnesses, forced to say to his children, ' I really will have mercy upon you, and will give you bread and butter.'

ALL THINGS OURS

Have you not noticed how little children stretch out their little hands for everything that comes within their reach ; for hard things or soft things, or even for the moon, as if all things were theirs, and as if they could accept and welcome all ? I have asked myself, Is not this instinct of a babe a sort of prophetic lesson for us, that all things are really ours ?

TWO WAYS OF LOVING

God is Love. But Love may be, and is, of two kinds—*Love in virtue of relationship*, and *Love in virtue of quality*. A father's or mother's love is an illustration of the first, which loves on unchanged, spite of the naughtiness, blindness, or madness of the loved one. A friend's or husband's love is the illustration of the second; for a friend or husband should choose his loved one according to quality; and with love of this kind, if the friend turns out a rogue, or if the wife is unfaithful, there follows a breach —the friendship is broken, and the wife is put away. Now, the first two Names of God in Genesis are given to reveal these two varying forms of love. In Elohim we have love according to, or in virtue of, relationship; in Jehovah, love in virtue of quality.

PRESENCE OF THE DEPARTED

I seem at times to have felt so really the presence of some at least of the departed, as we call them, that I find it hard to think of the outward court and the inward one as two distinct places. There is, I know, a veil between the two, for a short season—'the veil, that is to say, this flesh;' but it is already rent to faith, and before it is taken away it becomes, I think, sometimes transparent; and as we see through it or beyond it we see that the temple is really one, not two, and that those within and those without the veil are 'one Body.' If Christ is in us, the saints who are in Christ must also be in us. This may seem absurd, so long as we are tied by conceptions formed from this hard and outward sense-world. It will seem plain when in the Spirit we see how one inflows into another, where One is all, and all are One.

1886

UNCONSCIOUS SERVICE

I send you this note at once to tell you, who complain that you are sorry you do not more help your brethren, that I at least feel that you and your dear mother, by your love and sympathy and receptivity, do greatly help me, though you may not be conscious of it. And I may tell you, further, what I have long proved to be the truth, that our unconscious service is often the best that we render to any one. I suppose that the rose is hardly conscious how it delights others by the perfume it gives forth. I fancy the stars hardly know how many ships and wanderers they have guided and lighted on their weary journeys. I am sure the poor woman of Samaria little thought how she was refreshing Christ by receiving what He had to give. God is wounded in being rejected. God is gladdened when we receive Him. The lover is gladdened simply by being received, even as he is grieved by being rejected. So each member of the body, by its receiving as much as by its giving, serves the others. You do not think you serve me by receiving my poor words, yet you do really so serve

me. . . . The Buddhists say that a spiritual man
must be tested by his willingness to receive as to
give.

ORIGEN

I have great reverence for Origen, and owe him
many thoughts, especially as to Holy Scripture being
an Incarnation, and that it is the Divine Word in
creature form, and as it comes out of the heart of
man, that is, as man can receive it. For as it is
in itself, though so near us always, it is above the
apprehension of fallen carnal man.

VIRGINITY

How could you for a moment think I might ' scorn
or laugh at you ' for being exercised in heart as to the
virginity of those who win the prize of being the first-
fruits ? No one, I think, can have longed perfectly
to be conformed to Christ without at some time
having been led to ask what is the meaning of such
passages of Holy Scripture as those which you refer to.
The Church's history shows how deeply many have
felt on this subject ; for through many hundreds of
years, from earliest ages, thousands in every land
gave themselves up to live a virgin life, or at least to
attempt to live it, at all cost, in hope thereby more

to be conformed to Christ. For in those days the Church distinctly taught that a virgin life had special glories ; and even now in the Greek and Roman Churches, monasteries and nunneries show how the doctrine of the celibacy of the spiritual, or of those who wish to be spiritual, is accepted as a settled truth by the greater part of Christendom. It has only been since the Reformation, when the dreadful abuses which resulted from the attempt of unconverted men and women to live a celibate life made the very profession of it appear to be a downright lie and mockery, that any have questioned the old Church teaching as to poverty, chastity, and obedience being ' counsels of perfection ' for such as are ' able to receive them.' Protestantism and Protestants have much to answer for as to the way in which ' justification by faith alone ' has been preached and pressed against the old Catholic teaching of self-denial and self-sacrifice. I, at least, for more than forty years have had my heart exercised upon this question ; and I do not hesitate to say that I accept the old teaching as to the so-called ' counsels of perfection ; ' . . . for I think I see it distinctly taught by our Lord Himself in that section of the Gospel according to St. Matthew which follows His teaching as to the Church, ch. xvi. 13–xviii. 35 giving us seven great and distinctive truths as to

the Church, and then ch. xix.-xx. 29 distinctly teaching
the Evangelical 'counsels of perfection' to 'such as
can receive them;' for 'all men cannot receive these
sayings.'

But while I believe all this, and think that
Protestantism has suffered much from denying what
Scripture teaches so clearly, namely, that these two
are two stages in the Christian life, the carnal and
the spiritual, and that the one calls us to sacrifices
which at the other stage are simply impossible—
while, I say, I believe all this, I do not therefore
think that marriage, or the fact that a man has ever
had intercourse with any woman, cuts him off from
the highest prize to be won in Christ's kingdom.
For, if marriage is any hindrance to disciples ever
becoming parts of the Bride of Christ—in other words,
if the virginity spoken of in Rev. xiv. is virginity in
the flesh—then certainly St. Peter and other of the
Apostles who were married cannot win the prize; nor
can all the 'bishops and deacons' who, according to
St. Paul's direction, are to have wives, ever hope to
win that glory.   Nay, more, at this rate, St. Paul's
direction in 1 Cor. vii. 3-5, or St. Peter's exhortation
to husbands to 'dwell with their wives according to
knowledge' . . . would be a direct exhortation to
them to do that which would cut off souls from the

promised glory of being joint-heirs with Christ. I
think, therefore, that in the passage you refer to, it is
not virginity in the flesh which is spoken of, but
rather in the spirit. And the words in St. Luke xx.
34, 35, if I understand them, simply contrast this
present world with the coming resurrection. Here,
in this world, unless there is marriage the race would
soon die out: there, in the first resurrection, they
cannot die. Therefore marriage is not needed to continue the race. But one who in this world has been
married may reach the first resurrection, where
marriage is not needed; for in our resurrection-
bodies there is neither male nor female, the division
which exists here, and which was not in the beginning, being then done away.

I think, too, that such a verse as Rev. ii. 20,
where we read of ' teaching My servants to commit
fornication,' seems to show that the fornication
spoken of is spiritual; for what Church has ever
permitted fleshly fornication to be taught? Babylon,
the mother of harlots or harlotries, is, if I understand
it, the mother of spiritual harlotry. To be ' defiled
with women,' therefore, seems to me to be the same
as the adultery and fornication which Jeremiah,
Ezekiel, and St. James speak of, . . . namely, to
adulterate and falsify the truth; while to be a

'virgin' means to love the truth alone, and to be
waiting to be joined to the Lord ; as St. Paul says,
'I have espoused you to one Husband, that I may
present you as a chaste virgin to Christ.' . . .

While, then, I confess that chastity, poverty, and
obedience—and poverty as much as chastity—are
to be not accepted only but sought by those who wish
to be truly spiritual, I cannot say that those who are
married may not be virgins before God ; for cannot
we 'become as little children,' as our Lord teaches ?
and if we are such little children, must we not be also
virgins ? . . . Has the Church been wrong in teaching her children to sing the Blessed Virgin's song,
'*My* soul doth magnify the Lord.   And behold from
henceforth all generations shall call *me* blessed'? . . .

BAPTISMAL REGENERATION

As to regeneration, . . . brought up as I had been
among the Evangelicals of the Church of England,
I had great difficulties, when it pleased God to bring
me consciously to Himself, in receiving some of the
statements of the Prayer Book.   I had been taught
to regard regeneration and conversion as identical.
With such views, of course, the doctrine of the Prayer
Book seemed a mistake.   Was it not absurd to say
that unconscious babes are 'regenerate,' if regenera-

tion was indeed conversion ?   This difficulty I felt so
strongly that I declined to use the service, and so
for several years was practically an outcast from my
brethren.

But there were always two or three plain texts
which more or less raised another difficulty.   I had
been taught, and believed, that infants dying before
actual transgression could by grace be saved, and
therefore enter the kingdom of God and heaven.
And yet our Lord's reiterated 'Verily, verily,' distinctly asserted that 'except a man be born again,
he cannot see the kingdom of God.'   If, therefore,
children could enter heaven, they must somehow be
born again.   Then the statement of St. Peter struck
me, that 'God hath begotten us again . . . by the
resurrection of Jesus Christ from the dead;' seeming
to teach that as we died in Adam so we were made
alive in Jesus Christ.   And the language of Gal. iv.
seemed in the same direction, that 'because we are
sons, God hath sent the Spirit of His Son into our
hearts'—not (as I had been taught) that because God
hath sent the Spirit of His Son into our hearts, therefore we are sons.   We were 'heirs' when we were
'children, and in bondage under the elements of the
world.'   Then came my experience with my own
children, linked in my mind with St. Paul's statement

L

as to the Jews (the fleshly seed of a man of faith, I mean Abraham), that 'to them pertained the adoption, or sonship, and the promises '—a line of thought very specially forced on me when I had to teach my children how to pray, and by what name they should address God, and whether they might truly say, ' Our Father.'

Gradually one of the sayings of Charles Simeon, the leader of the old Evangelicals at Cambridge—that we should never perfectly understand the Gospel till we saw there were but two men, Adam and Christ, and that we were lost in the one and saved in the Other—came to me with fresh light, as showing that regeneration, even as degeneration, might be wrought for us, and that baptism might be the sign and witness of this accomplished regeneration.   Gradually I began to see, what I had always confessed, that as the most innocent child is degenerate in Adam, dead, ruined, helpless, lost, irrespective of any actual transgression committed by it, and even when to outward eyes it seems full of life and health, and manifests none of the distinctive ways or unbelief of old Adam, so the same child might be regenerate in Christ, irrespective of any good work wrought by it, and while as yet it manifested none of the distinctive works of faith of the New Man, our Lord Jesus.

Could Christ's work do less for us than Adam's? Of course, if baptism was the witness or token of the recipient's true conversion, no unconscious babe should or could ever be baptised. At this rate Simon Magus ought not to have been baptised. But if baptism was the sign of man's regeneration in Christ our Lord, and that through His grace we might at any age come to claim and apprehend that for which we are already apprehended, then the Church might be quite right in confessing over her children that, while they were all dead in Adam, they yet were quickened again in Jesus Christ, even though at the time they had no personal experience or consciousness of this regeneration.

One thing at least the Gospels seemed to teach, namely, that the faith of friends or parents obtained the very highest blessings for those whom they might bring to Christ—witness the Centurion and the Syrophenician woman, and many others. As I weighed all this, I could not but feel that the Church had not been so far wrong as I once thought in her doctrine of baptism.

FASTING BEFORE COMMUNION

I thought your paper the other day very telling, its tone and spirit as much as its facts. But I feel

L 2

(what, indeed, you allowed) that the rule you pressed
must have many exceptions in the case of the sick,
the aged, and the weak. If the Church's rule as to
fasting generally cannot be pressed on them either in
Lent or in the weekly fasts, can it be pressed in
reference to the Holy Communion? I used to fast
constantly and regularly, and at times severely. I
cannot do it now. If age has a certain dispensation,
so, I think, has poverty. Therefore, as I hinted, I
think Rom. xiv. 5, 6 has an application to the question.
At all events, we are not judges of our brethren. And
I say this while I feel with you how weighty is the
Church's judgment upon this question through so
many centuries.

1887

BABYLON

If, in my last hurried note, I seemed to say that
Babylon was exclusively Rome, I must have expressed
myself very carelessly. Babylon, to me, is something far wider than Romanism. ' In her was found
the blood of all that were slain upon the earth.'
She is that system of confusion, if confusion may be
called a system, which is the result of Lucifer's fallen

kingdom, and as such represents not so much any outward *place* as a certain *character*; and yet, because outward things are the manifestations of inward principles, outward persons and places may, and will, be partial and temporary manifestations of spiritual good and evil; and thus a city or a man may be the manifestation either of God or Satan. In this way Rome has been, I think, the City of confusion; though that City is far wider than Rome, and may include the Church of England, and every other system which confounds truth and falsehood, love and self-love. . . . The truth is, that in Roman Catholicism there are two distinct and different elements. There is the Catholic element, which is true, and the Roman element, which seems to me untrue. The sad thing is that, in practice, the Roman element, which is the lust of rule at all price, is put first; and what is true and good and catholic is too often misused to hold souls in bondage to what is merely Roman.

THE DEMONIAC BEYOND THE SEA

The healing of the demoniac ' on the other side' of the deep waters, which we all have to cross, is Divinely significant. On this side Christ heals leprosy, fever, palsy, and casts out devils, and frees us from the bonds of the dead old man, who must be

buried, if not by us.   Christ further is with us in
the storm as we cross the deep waters, but Christ does
more than this.   'On the other side' there are poor
souls, 'possessed by devils,' of whom it is said that
they are 'unclothed' and 'among the tombs,' and
miserable enough.   There is help even for such.   But
the Gospel for such as are 'unclothed' (in St. Paul's
sense of the word, 2 Cor. v. 4), and who are 'coming
out of the tombs,' though it is Gospel, is hardly for
all, at least during this life.

FOUR WAYS OF KNOWING

According to the old Church view there are four
different ways of knowing anything, figured by the
four streams of the one river which flowed forth from
Paradise.   We may know a thing, first, *on testimony*,
that is, by being told of it.   This is to fallen creatures
the first way of knowing the love of Christ.   Again,
we may know a thing *by reasoning it out*.   In this
way, too, we may know the love of Christ, by reasoning
that, if we that are evil will give good gifts to our
children, how much more will Christ, who is the
image of the invisible God, give good things even to
His lost and wandering creatures?   Again, we may
know a thing *by feeling it*, or by sense.   I suppose
we have all known the difference between knowing the

love of Christ by being told of it and by feeling it. This third way of knowing is experimental, and full of comfort to those who by grace possess it. But there is a fourth way of knowing anything, the intuitive way, which comes by *having the thing itself*. This is the way of ways to know Christ's love—yourself to have it—so to live that it is not you that live, but Christ Himself who lives in you, and who, because He lives in you, loves all with His own love.

THE IDEAL CHURCH

Mr. H. speaks, and speaks truly, of the ideal Church, that is, of the Church as it is and shall be in our Lord Jesus Christ. His words remind me of the wonderfully beautiful words respecting the 'Church which was in the wilderness,' as seen by the prophet in vision when he said, 'How goodly are thy tents, O Jacob, and thy tabernacles, O Israel. . . . He hath not beheld iniquity in Jacob, neither hath He seen perverseness in Israel. The Lord his God is with him, and the shout of a King is among them.' This is the Church according to God's purpose, as seen in His dear Son. But there is another side of the same picture, as all the faithful prophets teach, who see not only God's purpose but the Church's sin, and who in God's Spirit say, 'Hear the word of the Lord, ye

rulers of Sodom : give ear unto the law of our God,
ye people of Gomorrah.   To what purpose is the
multitude of your sacrifices unto Me ?   Bring no more
vain oblations ; incense is an abomination unto Me :
it is iniquity, even the solemn meeting.'   Nay, even
more, 'As I live, saith the Lord God, Sodom thy
sister hath not done, she nor her daughters, as thou
hast done, thou and thy daughters.'   I cannot understand Matt. xxiv. if Israel's history and end is not
a shadow and figure of the spiritual Israel.   Christ
in the flesh was slain by the seed of Abraham in
the flesh.   Christ in the spirit is rejected, and, if
I err not, will be still more rejected, by the seed of
Abraham in the spirit.   It seems to me that the
state of Israel of old when our Lord came answered
very nearly to the Church's state in these days.
Ten   tribes   had   long   been   lost.   Samaria   was
practically apostate.   The 'land of Zebulon and
Naphtali'   had   become   'Galilee of the Gentiles.'
Only in Jerusalem did they preserve the true order
and succession of the priesthood.   Yet in Jerusalem
was our Lord crucified, while He lived a Galilean and
ate in Samaria.   All this is an awful voice to me.
Like Daniel, I have been 'astonied, and there has
remained no strength in me.'   But, like the same

Daniel, I believe that you and I and many more by grace 'shall rest and stand in our lot at the end of the days.'

THE APOCALYPSE

It has for years been clear to me that none of the three popular schools of interpretation—I mean the Continuously Historical, the Futurist, or the Præterist—. . . .can possibly be the true, or at least the full, solution of the mystery of the Apocalypse. It is, what its opening title declares it to be, '*the Revelation* (or unveiling) *which God gives to Jesus Christ*,' showing the way in which the life of God is manifested in the fallen creature in body, soul, and spirit, through varied and successive judgments; for it is only by a succession of meltings and transmutations that, in the creature's renewal unto God, the Divine Life, growing out of, and for a season linked to, an earthly fallen nature, is dissolved and purified till it is seen as perfectly immortal. Dr. Milligan has in a measure grasped this idea; but he would, I think, have seen it even more clearly had he received the truth that the self-same 'revelation' is being fulfilled in each individual soul and body, and that for every one of us the process is the same; the general law of God's dispensations, which is more or less confessed in the

outward world, having its fulfilment in every particular in the kingdom of God which is within us.

HEALTH

There is no secret of health and recovery like a
heart which with all its failings rests on God. Fear
is the certain cause of disease : faith and hope the
certain cause of recovery, even for these poor dying
bodies.

1888

THE DEATH OF LORD MOUNT TEMPLE

The world, the seen world, must henceforth be
colder to us. But what is real never passes away.
We cannot lose what we truly love. And the love of
which Broadlands has been a centre and witness will
never leave us. The departed are still very near us,
though we may not see them. And Lady Mount
Temple will be supported, and know perhaps as she
has never known the love of him whose love has been
through a lifetime so much to her. I am exceedingly
sure that our Lord's words touching Himself, 'It is
expedient for you that I go away,' are true of all those
to whom to live is Christ. Through their outward

departure we get, even from them or through them, what
we never got while they were with us visibly.   Surely
they yet are with us.   'We *are come* to the spirits of
just men made perfect.' . . . Yet I feel the chill and
the blank the last few days have made.   How many
others too will feel it.

1889

BLESSED ARE THE MOURNERS

I can tell you for an eternal truth that troubled
souls are always safe.   It is the untroubled that are
in danger.   Trouble in itself is always a claim on
love, and God is love.   He must deny Himself if He
does not come to help the helpless.   It is the pri-
soners, and the blind, and the leper, and the possessed,
and the hungry, and the tempest-tossed, who are His
special care.   Therefore, if you are lost and sick and
bound, you are just in the place where He can meet
you.   Blessed are the mourners.   They shall be
comforted.

As to your special perplexity and distress, it may
arise from any one of many causes.   I do not know
what you have been going through.   But I know
that a serpent's bite, or a scorpion's sting, or a
poisoned cup, or even unwholesome food, or over-

work, or anxiety, may all cause the body sharpest pain.
Just so may the temptation of a poisoned word or
thought distress and sting the soul, and cause it for
days or months or years the sharpest anguish. Some,
indeed, not many, can take up serpents and any
deadly thing unhurt. Most men suffer from such
things. But the joy for sufferers is that the very
suffering must in the long run work for good. We
should never have been allowed to come into a world
of pain had not perfect Wisdom seen that suffering
and death could be made not only the remedy for all
our ills, but even the means to bring us to a higher
and securer glory. Therefore, whatsoever the trouble,
rest in the Lord. And if you cannot rest, then in all
your restlessness and doubt, be the darkness what it
may, sink down and down till you come to the everlasting Arms which are underneath us all, and which
will surely bring you up in due season. And as a
remedy which cannot fail, say often, and say always,
' Lord Jesus! Lord Jesus! ' and you will find that
there is a magic in the words. . . . He who writes
this can say, ' A day and a night I have been in
the deep,' yea, I have been swallowed up like Jonah,
and felt as if ' hell with her bars were around me
for ever ; ' and proved that this is the way of life, the
one appointed way.

REVIVALISM

I should try to show some special kindness to the girl, and rather press on her some good thing, such as more prayer, which her conscience will feel is surely right, than enter into any protests against this or that particular error which the so-called Revivalist has encouraged in the parish.   These exciting doings are really like an attack of measles or some other infectious disease in a family.   They are very catching.   But they pass away, though sometimes not without the loss of a dear child.   The best way of meeting such an epidemic is by keeping the patients warm by very kind and tender ministry of love.   The fever then runs its course sooner. . . . Be like a nurse, tenderly nourishing the sufferers.   You will get them all back by love.   And be not over-anxious.   All these things are in God's hands.

THE ROMAN CHURCH

All you tell me of the Roman or Spanish services and ceremonies of ' Holy Week ' was more or less familiar to me. . . . It is all carnal and in the flesh, and not what our souls need; yet it is not perhaps more carnal than the slaying of oxen, and the washing of their inward parts, and the burning of their flesh

or dung, and the washing of hands or vestments, all
of which were once appointed for a carnal people, by
the self-same God whom we now worship in spirit, to
be some shadow of the great sacrifice and of the great
purification which is wrought for us by the outpouring
of the precious blood of the Blessed Lamb of God.
You may say that these things were appointed of old
because the time for better things had not yet come,
and men were in the flesh, and God therefore stooped
to meet men where they were. This is true. But
what God once does He is ever doing for souls in a
like state. He never changes. And therefore there
may not be so great a mistake as some dear brethren
think in these carnal presentations of the great facts
of the great sacrifice in a land and among a people
very few of whom are prepared by grace for better
things. This is a very deep subject, though some,
who by grace have been brought out of the darkness
into the light, speak as if the shadows and even the
darkness for a while were a mistake. But God makes
no mistakes. The 'shadows' surely have their place,
and the carnal service was a 'shadow;' and even the
'darkness' has its use. Souls may be brought into
light too soon, and, like unborn babes brought forth
from the womb before their time, may suffer lifelong
weakness through the haste of those who do not see

that 'there is a time and season' for everything.
Think of the Eternal Son, the Word, the Light of the
world, waiting all those ages before He gave even the
Law; and then again waiting all those other ages
till he gave the Gospel. Think how He sent John
the Baptist with one message, and then came Himself with yet another. Think how He came in the
flesh, under a veil, before He comes in the Spirit.
Think how, when He came in the flesh of Jesus of
Nazareth, though ' He had many things to say,' He
did not say them. Think of His reserve with even
His disciples, and His reserve with us : how He allows
years and years to pass—their whole lifetime here with
some dear brethren—before He opens to them fully
the meaning of the very words which are their
strength and comfort. It is all a loud voice to me,
though there is no speech which men hear. . . . You
may perhaps say, Carnal ceremonies and shadows
were permitted in Judaism, but now the great Sacrifice
has been made, and shadows and carnal forms are
not now permissible. Do you say this ? I know
some say so. Of such I ask, When did the Sacrifice of
the Lamb of God begin ? Was He, or was He not,
' the Lamb slain from the foundation of the world ' ?
If the Old Testament saints had the Divine life
renewed in them (and you will hardly deny this),

how could they get that life but by the outpouring of
the ' blood of the Lamb of God ' ? for ' the blood is
the life.' Do you say, They got that Divine life by the
Word of God, for the Word is the seed, which quickens
God's life in man ? If you say this you are right.
But all seed, whether of God or man or beast or
plant, is the essence of the blood or life. And the
Lamb of God, from the foundation of the world,
and from the Fall, was pouring out for us His life, that
as many as receive it should again receive God's
life, and in that life obey and please God. The
blessed Incarnation of the Blessed Lord was an outward and visible sign of an eternal truth, even of the
truth that God was giving His life to men, by which
death should be conquered, and man be brought out
of his fall to God's right hand, to be His heir and
first-born in restoring and reconciling all.

PRAYERS FOR THE DEPARTED

I know many good people think it wrong to pray
for the dead. I was brought up in this tradition, but
I believe it is merely a tradition of men, and has
nothing to justify it in Holy Scripture or reason. It
is at least certain that the Jews of old used to pray
for the dead, and yet our Lord never said a word
against this practice, though He corrected other

mistakes as to prayer. . . . It is quite certain that the early Christian Church used to pray for the dead. . . . In the Communion Service we pray that ' we and all Thy whole Church may obtain remission of our sins, and all other benefits of Christ's passion ; ' and surely ' Thy whole Church ' must include the departed. . . . It seems to me that nature itself teaches us to pray for the dead. Who is there who has lost a dearly loved one, who has not followed that loved one with thanksgiving and prayers ? At all events, it is many long years, more than thirty, since, in spite of all my Protestant bringing up, I have felt constrained to pray for the departed. . . . For though they are, I believe, at peace, I cannot say that they are yet perfect ; and I pray for their perfection.

PATIENCE WITH THE YOUNG : ALL SOULS

Of course your hands will be full of work, and your heart full of cares, as you move about among these boys and girls who are now your charge. But you need not be anxious, for the Lord Himself cares for them. While they are children they must think as children and speak as children. I would not have it otherwise. There is an appointed time for that which is first and natural ; and we are not wise if we try to hasten the bringing forth of what is spiritual

M

before its proper time. Think how God has waited with mankind for ages, and how He has waited with us for years, bearing our manners till the fullness of the time was come for the new man to be quickened and brought forth out of the old. Let us also learn to bear with those who are yet unfit for the best things. As to All Saints' Day, with you I rejoice to think of the loved ones who are at rest, who have finished their course here, and are with Him they loved. To-day, too, All Souls' Day, is a precious day to me. . . . I can rejoice, and do rejoice, that all souls are yet the Lord's, and that the day is coming when they shall be seen to be the inheritance of the Lord and of His chosen.

WAR AND SUFFERING

There can be no question as to the awfulness of the acts and scenes referred to. But the real question which faces us is not, Are such things awful? but rather, Why do they exist, and why are they permitted, if there is a God, and if God is really the Ruler of the universe? Is it or is it not true that not a sparrow falls to the ground without His knowledge? And yet, is it not an awful fact that disease and madness and death are on every hand? Do they come by chance, or are they the result and manifestation of something yet more terrible than the worst suffering in this world? Surely the real evil is not pain or suffering, but sin. The suffering, terrible as it is, is God's means to free man from the real evil. Therefore, so long as sin remains, its punishment, whether by disease or war, terrible as the punishment is to flesh and blood, is real mercy. Which was really worse, the sin of Sodom, or the judgment which brought the iniquity to an end? Which was worse, the sin of Israel, or 'the sword, the famine, and the pestilence' which cut off old and young, and so put a stop to their pollutions and idolatries? God forbid that England should be invaded; but if, for our sins, London should be sacked, and the streets filled, as Jerusalem was filled, with corpses innumerable, which would be the real evil—the sin which brought the judgment, or the judgment which, whenever it comes, comes to make the evil cease? Of course, the innocent suffer not only with the guilty, but for the guilty. This is the great mystery of the Cross. But there is no mistake in it. A sinful world without suffering would be the great mistake. Some day sin will be done away. But it is yet in the world; and while there is sin there must be judgment.

HOLY MATRIMONY

[Ingersoll's book] seems to show that, on your side of the Atlantic, the thoughts even of educated men and women as to the marriage-union are very different from those of most people in this country. In England, marriage is called and is regarded as ' Holy Matrimony ' . . . the marriage-union being the earthly figure of the union of God and man, of which Christ, our Blessed Lord, is the witness and sacrament. Of course, as St. Paul says to Titus, while ' to the pure all things are pure,' ' to them that are undefiled and unbelieving nothing is pure, but even their mind and conscience are defiled.' Just, then, as some of the impure Gnostics of old held and taught that God could not really come in the flesh, because such coming in the flesh, they thought, would be defilement, so impure souls may still think the marriage-bond, which is the figure of God's union with our nature even in its present separation, is unclean also. The Church has always protested against such a denial of the truth ; and St. Paul's words (1 Tim. iv. 1–4) show us his thoughts, which are the thoughts of God, on this subject.

THE WINE-PRESS

Augustine dwells much on the lesson of the wine-press, which seems to crush out not only the beauty of the grape, but all its sweetness also, leaving to be seen only some tasteless skins ; but which through this very process brings the juice, or life, into another place and another form, where it will no longer feel the frost, or be preyed upon by the caterpillar, but where it will make glad the heart of God and man as it never did in its first verdant earthly beauty, and where it will be rectified and purified, so that it cannot see corruption.

1890

'LUX MUNDI' AND INSPIRATION

Gore's essay . . . I have twice read, and both times carefully. The earlier part of it is very good —some portions of it beautiful. The latter part, as to the Inspiration of Holy Scripture, seemed to me not 'incautious' only, but unsatisfactory, confounding between Inspiration and its results, and, while clearly bringing out the human side of Holy Scripture, not sufficiently emphasising its real Divinity. This, if I am right in my estimate of this part of the essay, is

surely a defect. For as, in reference to our Blessed
Lord, the Council of Nicæa, with its ἀληθῶς ('truly
God'), was needed as much as the Council of Constantinople with its τέλεως ('perfectly man'), so the
real Divinity of Holy Scripture is as much to be
contended for as its true and perfect humanity—more
to be contended for, perhaps, in these days when
rationalism is practically pushing God out of His own
world, occupied with the wonderful beauty of what is
His work, but seeing in it the work rather than the
Worker. Gore's essay . . . seemed to err in this
direction, and, as I thought, also to lack precision of
thought and language. Take for instance his words
in pp. 343–4. He asks, 'What is meant by the
Inspiration of Holy Scripture?' and then, after
speaking of what the Bible contains, he says, ' These
are the fundamental principles of true religion and
progressive morality, and in these *lies* the supernatural
inspiration of the Bible,' &c. Had he said, ' In these
is manifested its supernatural inspiration,' one
could not object. But in p. 351 he again repeats the
same thought and the same word: ' The inspiration of
the recorder *lies primarily* in this, that he sees the
hand of God in the history.' Does the inspiration
really ' lie ' in this, or is it not rather ' manifested ' in
this? . . . The words, too, on p. 346, that 'the

prophetic inspiration is thus consistent with erroneous anticipations,' seem to me similarly imperfect and uncertain. If they only mean that prophetic inspiration may co-exist with imperfect understanding and interpretation in the prophet, they may of course be true ; for, as St. Peter tells us, ' the prophets searched what, or what manner of time the Spirit which was in them did signify, when it testified beforehand the sufferings of Christ, and the glory that should follow ; ' but Mr. Gore seems to mean more than this, even that the prophecies themselves were ' erroneous anticipations.' Is not the truth this rather, that the prophets, though speaking in the Spirit, failed to take in or understand the perfect sense of what they truly saw or uttered ? . . .

I am writing more than I intended. But to me, such an essay as C. Gore's, from the Head of the Pusey House, is a sign of what is coming and must come. Holy Scripture must as surely be rejected by professing Christendom before the end comes, because of its perfect humanity, as the Christ was by the Jew because, being in the flesh, He claimed to be the Son of God. But even thus, now as of old, spite of the sin, man will be led on from what is seen and outward to the wider opening of another world and of still more direct communion with it.

THE HOLY SPIRIT'S HOME-COMING

We don't expect half enough from Him. If the evil spirit is so ready to return to what he calls 'his house,' with seven other spirits more wicked than himself, what will the Holy Spirit do, if only we can 'wait for the promise of the Father'? Will He not come with all His sevenfold power, to turn carnal disciples, who have only known Christ in the flesh, to do His works and minister His Spirit as they have never done before? Shall the evil, selfish, hellish spirit do more for his slaves than the Spirit of God does for His own children?

ALL SAINTS AND ALL SOULS

Touching All Saints' Day and All Souls' Day, it is true that All Souls was originally intended to refer to the baptised, who as such might be regarded as 'the faithful,' that is, 'believers' in Christ, though their lives had been such that they missed the prize of being numbered among All Saints. But if such souls could and should be prayed for, who can be excluded from our prayers? for there is no sin so great as the sin of those who, having been baptised, live godless lives. . . . The Church, with her faithful and unfaithful members, is a witness of God's purpose towards all.

PRAYERS FOR ALL MEN

As to prayers 'for all men,' I have not a doubt about them. None are out of God's hand, or beyond His reach. All Souls' Day has for many years seemed to me an opportunity for reminding or teaching people on this point; though strictly speaking the Festival of All Souls was originally intended for those of the baptised whose lives showed that they in no true sense were 'All Saints.' The Church, like all the prophets, has often taught more than she understood. St. Peter on the Day of Pentecost preached about the Spirit being poured out upon all flesh, and yet very slowly apprehended even after this that a Gentile could be baptised. It is not every true believer, [nor] even every saint, who to-day has learnt what the 'great sheet let down from heaven' taught Peter—'God hath shown me that I should call no man common or unclean.'

1891

REDEMPTION. FOUR GREAT TEACHERS

Redemption (as Coleridge says somewhere in a book, 'Aids to Reflection,' which in my time was much read at Cambridge) is brought before us in St. Paul's epistles, or in the New Testament, under several distinct aspects, as sacrifice, or ransom, or satisfaction, or reconciliation—the last view being rather atonement than redemption. I have long thought that the old view, of the ransom being paid to Satan, though stated ridiculously by some of the early Fathers, is nearer to the truth than the view put forth, if I remember right, by Anselm in his ' Cur Deus Homo,' that the ransom was paid by the Son to the Father : which ended in the monstrous perversion that the Father held us captive and the Son freed us, which has been the creed of not a few Protestants. What Scripture says is that we are ' ransomed from the grave,' and ' redeemed from the enemy,' as Israel was of old from Egypt ; that therefore it is evil, or death, or sin, or Satan that held us captive, and that from this captivity we are delivered or bought back ' by the blood of the Son,' that is, the life, so freely given and poured out for us, which frees us from our bonds, and makes atonement also, so that we are not only redeemed from bondage but brought into communion with God also. . . .

All Law's works have for years been on my shelves and in my hands. He is one of the three men who, more than any others outside the Bible, have helped me ; the other two being Augustine and F. D. Maurice.

Perhaps I ought to name a fourth—I refer to Origen. To him also I am a great debtor. He, too, as you know, holds that the ransom was paid to—that is, that we were redeemed from—Satan.

CHRIST AND PAGAN FORMS

The Tract calls attention to a question which has often, and especially in early days, occupied Christians, namely, whether the worship and traditions of the old world, both Jewish and heathen, were or were not originally 'shadows of the true;' and, further, whether He who came into our fallen form and into our flesh, to fill it with another life, can or cannot fill all forms, whether Jewish or heathen, with His Spirit, if only He comes and takes possession of them. The question is not whether our fallen form or nature has or has not been perverted, and for years possessed by Satan, but whether Christ and His Spirit can come into those forms, once filled by Satan, and fill them with His own Spirit. Two answers were given to this question in early days—one, the Puritan answer; the other, the Catholic. Marcion (I think it was Marcion, but my memory fails) and many others, who took the Puritan line, said that not only all heathen forms, but Jewish also, were all of them from the devil—that the God of the Jews, who commanded white raiment, and the blood of beasts, and fleshly cleansings, could not be our God, for all such forms were evil; and that as to the heathen traditions, of the woman and child, and of a virgin-born deliverer, and of the purification of the mother, or nature, which bore the man-child, and of the cross or Tau, which figured perfection; and of the serpent lifted up upon a pole, and of the resurrection of the deliverer, who had many names, and that spring, when all nature is bursting with life, was the time of his resurrection, as winter, when days are darkest, was of his coming into the world; and that the Saturnalia, the feast which said that all men once were brothers, and that masters should serve servants, and servants act as masters—that all these things were not only vile pagan superstitions, but were invented by the devil as caricatures of what God was going to do in Christ, and only invented to keep men from Christ and His salvation. On the other hand, there were other teachers (and the Church generally accepted their view) who held that Christ's Incarnation, or coming into our form and nature, spite of man's perversions of that form and nature, was the witness that He could cleanse everything—that as our fallen nature, in its first form, came from God, so the Jewish and heathen forms, however fallen and

corrupted, had once been figures of eternal verities
—in a word, that both the heathen and Jewish
tradition was originally true, the Jewish more perfect,
but the heathen also wonderful ; who therefore,
instead of saying that the ceremonial law of Moses
came from an evil spirit, tried to show that it all
pointed to Christ ; and who in like manner saw even
in the heathen traditions a shadow, perhaps less perfect
than the Jewish shadows, of the same old traditions
which had come down from Adam and Noah, that ' the
Seed of the woman should bruise the serpent's head.'
These brethren therefore thought that Paul was right
in ' becoming a Jew to gain the Jews,' and that
indeed he was only doing what God and Christ had
done, for Christ too was circumcised and kept the law
before heaven opened to Him at His baptism.

The Tract you have sent me shows that there are
still some who are so shocked and offended by the old-
world forms that they do not see the truth which
once lay under them, and that to the pure all things
are pure, while to the defiled and unbelieving nothing
is pure. St. Paul could say that even ' an idol is
nothing in the world,' even while he saw that others
' with conscience of the idol ' are ' defiled ' and stumbled
by it. It seems to me (though I may be wrong) that
a person's ' conscience ' must be ' weak ' indeed who

thinks that now in England we are in danger of
' Tammuz and Nimrod and Saturn,' or that it is wrong
and perilous to say, ' Saturday, Sunday, Monday, or
Tuesday,' because all these names are the names of
heathen gods. Is any one really hurt by calling ·
March 25 ' Lady Day ' ?   But you cannot make men's
minds or consciences alike.   Some, like flies, light on
sores and dunghills : some, like bees, get honey from
every flower.   Both have their use in this world.
But I think if we could be more like Him who came in
the flesh to bring His life and Spirit into it we might
more serve others.   All, however, have their own
gift, one after this manner, another after that.

1892

CHURCH AND DISSENT

The question you ask is, ' Granted that the Church,
spite of its fall and division, is one, what ought to be
the relation of the Church to Dissent ? '   By ' Church '
here you mean, I suppose, the Church of England.
Shall I answer this with another question ?   What
was, or ought to have been, the relation of Jerusalem,
in our Lord's day, to Galilee, or Samaria, or to the
dispersed Jews scattered through Pontus, Galatia,

and Cappadocia ? Jerusalem had the Temple with
its priests and the appointed service, though without
the Ark. It was the Divinely ordained centre for
true worship. Galileans and Samaritans, the mixed
children of the ten tribes, were in more or less
schism and darkness. What was to be done ? Could
any one unite divided Samaria, Galilee, and Jerusalem ? Did our Lord attempt it ? Or was it His
work to bring in and manifest the heavenly life,
which would make not only Jews and Galileans one,
but which would also make Jew and Gentile, that
is, Church and world, 'a new creature' ? Christ's
way and life and death, if we ever really see it, are
the answer to your question. I, at least, cannot
imagine how, as outward organisations, the Church
of England can be united with the various divisions
and constantly increasing splits of Dissenters, who
now, even to the last new sect or split, are claiming
to be independent Churches. What the divided unite
to do is always a sham. The Dissenters are divided
and separate from the Church of England, and are
doing what they can to ruin it, as they think, by
disestablishment. Can you join them in this work ?
I once thought Dissent was a religious thing. It was
so at first. The sin of the Church in former years
almost forced true hearts and tender consciences into

separation and dissent from her. Even in my young
days, Dissent was to a great extent religious, though
mixed with not a little self-will. Now it is everywhere mainly social and political. . . . Political power
is sought at all costs, even by alliance with Romanists
and infidels, if only the Church of England can be
pulled down, as they think, by disestablishment. Of
course, disestablishment is coming, in the State as
much as in the Church. Universal anarchy and lawlessness are almost at the doors. The timid cling to
the old thing. But the things which are must go.
Still your question asks an answer, What is the right
course under such circumstances ? My answer again is
only Christ's life. What shall we do but, like the
Lord, be sacrifices for all, seeking to minister Christ's
Spirit to those who will receive it, and to the end
praying for all, that the promised end may come in
due season.

JUDGMENT: CAPITAL PUNISHMENT

Is it wrong to execute a malefactor ? Are we
right in taking the life of a man like N., who was
hanged the other day ? I say, Yes, certainly. God
and His angels judge, and judgment is right, and
we too shall judge some day. And it is not right
only, but it is mercy also, not to the world or

society only, but even to the malefactor. I do not hesitate to say with St. Ambrose (in his book ' De Bono Mortis ') that ' it is better to die in sin than to live in sin.' Still more evident is it to me that it is better for a malefactor to be judged here than to be unjudged, and so to go unpunished into the spirit world, for punished he must be, sooner or later ; and, as St. Peter says, ' He that hath suffered in the flesh hath ceased from sin.' Death puts an end to some part of the evil in a sinner. Death is no mistake or real evil in a fallen world. It is the way out of it. Is God's sending the sword or famine or pestilence wrong? Certainly not. ' The Lord killeth and maketh alive.' It is one part of His wondrous work ' by death to destroy him that hath the power of death,' and so to bring some evil to an end.

As to the fact that men and women with lusts, like Samson, treachery, like Jael, and lying, like Rahab, can yet by faith do wonders, he must know nothing of the world or of himself who doubts it. Some of the very best men have had the vilest natures, and even in seeking to serve God, and actually in serving Him, have done some of the vilest things ; and yet, through all their faults, faith has been their strength. What mistakes have I not made? What wretched things have I not done?

N

What a want of perfect truth and love in little words and little things there has been in me too often, even while my most earnest desire has been to serve God. When all secrets are made known, what will not be seen, even in some of the most faithful of the saints. Paul knew that he was 'chief of sinners.' No flesh shall glory—no, not even the best. This may seem incredible till we know the hidden world within us. Ask any old Christian . . . and he will tell you what awful confusions, spite of their faith, have often been within: the result of the fact that earth and heaven and hell, and flesh and spirit, are all in conflict in us.

1893

WHAT IS THE CHURCH?

My feeling is that it is almost, if not quite, impossible to answer the question, *What is the Church?* in a single statement. For the Church is Christ's Body; and it needed four Gospels, differing in many respects, to bring before us Who and What Christ is. Even to show us His sacrifice you need the Passover in Egypt, and the sweet-savour and non-sweet-savour offerings when out of Egypt. And just as there were different stages in the life of Christ,

in the flesh and in the spirit, as a babe, and young
man before heaven opened to Him, and as a victor
over Satan after this experience, so must it be with
His Body the Church. The early stages of Christ's
life were Jewish. Therefore He was circumcised,
and to the end of His earthly life here kept the Passover. Must it not be so with His Body the Church?
Must we not, though Gentiles, be 'grafted into the
Jewish olive-tree,' from which we may and must at
last be broken off? I have more than once greatly
scandalised both parties in our Church meetings . . .
by asking, When did our Lord become a Christian?
Was it Christian to be circumcised, and to be pre-
sented in the Temple? The answers to this question
which I have received at some of our clerical meetings would astonish you. Some have said, Christ
was *always* a Christian. Some have positively held
that He was *never* a Christian. And when I have
asked how this last view can possibly be true, seeing
that we are only Christians as 'Christ is formed in
us,' I have been told that all this is 'dreamy
mysticism.' Mysticism or no, I believe that when
Christ is first 'formed in us' He is unseen as the
Babe in Mary's womb was unseen when Elisabeth
greeted her—that at this stage what the outward eye
sees is only the nature which has received the Word

and Spirit, from which in due time the New Man is brought forth ; and that, even when so brought forth as to be seen separate from the mother or nature which has borne Him, the New Man is, and must be, yet bound by Jewish swaddling-clothes. All this and much more to the same effect is true of Christ. But, because it is true of Christ, it must be true of the Church which is His Body. How can you make this clear to carnal souls? You may 'speak wisdom among them that are perfect,' as St. Paul did; but with the mass even of converted men, who are carnal like the Corinthians, you must, if you are like St. Paul, determine to 'know nothing among them' save the great lesson of the Cross.

SPIRITISM

The question which you ask me is a difficult one. It seems to me that the answer depends not a little on the past history and present spiritual state of the lady who asks your guidance. Had she not been, as you say, 'much mixed up with spiritism,' the answer would, I think, be easier. If the spirit-world opens to us according to the will of God, independent of our self-will and carnal attempts to enter it, then, as it seems to me, the communications which we receive thence are not dangerous, but often may be most blessed, as in the case of the visions granted to our Lord in the days of His flesh, and to His apostles and prophets. A Divine Life, as it seems to me, cannot but open heaven. But to have attempted in worldliness and self-will to pass through the veil, and to have succeeded in measure in doing so, may, I think, leave results upon the organisation of the inquirer which cannot easily be shaken off. Thus the communications which have recently come to Miss Z. may be—I do not say they are—the necessary results of her bygone action. The reason you suggest as perhaps justifying Miss Z. in accepting, if not in seeking, these spirit-communications, is that to refuse to do so might show a want of love towards one who is struggling towards a knowledge of God ; while on the other hand the accepting of these communications might show love. This was the ground upon which one beloved and beautiful friend of mine justified intercourse with spirits, even granting that they might be devils. 'Ought we not,' she said, 'to run some risk to serve them if they are miserable ?' My fearful heart thought rather of the prophet's words, 'To obey is better than sacrifice.'

1894

FACT, FAITH, EXPERIENCE

We have in Rom. vi. 8–14 three things : fact, faith, and experience, as to our death and resurrection in and with the Lord. St. Paul begins with the fact as wrought for us in Christ : 'Christ being raised from the dead dieth no more, death hath no more dominion over Him. For in that He died, He died unto sin once : but in that He liveth, He liveth unto God.' All this is fact—all certain fact, fact wrought for us in Him Who came into our nature and took our place for us ; in Whom we were reconciled and redeemed before we were born, even as before we were born we fell in old Adam. . . . The apostle then goes on from fact to faith, faith in the fact wrought for us : 'Likewise reckon yourselves to be dead unto sin, but alive unto God in Jesus Christ our Lord.' This reckoning ourselves to be dead and alive again in Christ is simply faith—believing what has been done for us, which gives full peace with God, though we may be, and are, yet most imperfect. Then comes the experience, when that which was wrought for us in the Person of Christ as to death to sin and life to God is step by step by the same Spirit wrought in us also. So the apostle goes on again, ' Let not sin, therefore, reign in your mortal body to obey it, but yield yourselves unto God, and your members as instruments of righteousness unto God; ' even as Christ your Head and Life did in everything.

SORROW TURNED INTO JOY

Christ's Cross is the witness that God's dearest children must suffer, and there is a sacrificial use in our sufferings as well as in Christ's. In them we fill up what is wanting of the sufferings of Christ; and God Himself, our Father, also shares our troubles with us, for in all our afflictions He is afflicted. This mystery of present pain is to some a riddle they cannot solve, but I feel sure that sorrow is the very stuff that joy is made of. So our Lord says, ' Your sorrow shall be turned into joy.' He does not say, You shall have no sorrow; but ' Your sorrow shall be turned into joy,' as milk is turned into butter, which you cannot have without the milk. I once believed this, but now I know it.

PATIENCE

' The life is the light.' Live the truth; and, as you can bear it, all things you can bear will open to you.   You may rush into the spirit-world before you are fit for it, and only suffer loss by it.

1895

PEARLS

Have you ever noticed that all the Gates into the Heavenly City are Pearls ?   Do you know how pearls are formed ? that they are all the result of the suffering and disease of the poor little mollusk in whose shell they grow.   Oh, what ' pearls ' are coming, and are now forming, out of our daily sufferings.

PRINTED BY
SPOTTISWOODE AND CO. LTD., NEW-STREET SQUARE
LONDON

A Selection of Works

IN

THEOLOGICAL LITERATURE

PUBLISHED BY

Messrs. LONGMANS, GREEN, & CO.

London : 39 Paternoster Row, E.C.

New York : 91 and 93 Fifth Avenue.

Bombay : 32 Hornby Road.

Abbey and Overton.—THE ENGLISH CHURCH IN THE EIGHTEENTH CENTURY. By Charles J. Abbey, M.A., Rector of Checkendon, Reading, and John H. Overton, D.D., Canon of Lincoln. *Crown 8vo. 7s. 6d.*

Adams.—SACRED ALLEGORIES. The Shadow of the Cross—The Distant Hills—The Old Man's Home—The King's Messengers. By the Rev. William Adams, M.A. With Illustrations. *16mo. 3s. net.*

The four Allegories may be had separately, *16mo. 1s. each.*

Aids to the Inner Life.

Edited by the Venble. W. H. Hutchings, M.A., Archdeacon of Cleveland, Canon of York, Rector of Kirby Misperton, and Rural Dean of Malton. *Five Vols. 32mo, cloth limp, 6d. each ; or cloth extra, 1s. each.*

OF THE IMITATION OF CHRIST. By Thomas à Kempis.

THE CHRISTIAN YEAR.

THE DEVOUT LIFE. By St. Francis de Sales.

THE HIDDEN LIFE OF THE SOUL. By Jean Nicolas Grou.

THE SPIRITUAL COMBAT. By Laurence Scupoli.

Arbuthnot.—SHAKESPEARE SERMONS. Preached in the Collegiate Church of Stratford-on-Avon on the Sundays following the Poet's Birthday, 1894-1900. Collected by the Rev. George Arbuthnot, M.A., Vicar of Stratford-on-Avon. *Crown 8vo. 2s. 6d. net.*

Baily-Browne.—Works by A. B. Baily-Brown.

A HELP TO THE SPIRITUAL INTERPRETATION OF THE PENITENTIAL PSALMS, consisting of Brief Notes from The Fathers, gathered from Neale and Littledale's Commentary. With Preface by the Rev. George Body, D.D., Canon of Durham. *Crown 8vo. 1s. net.*

THE SONGS OF DEGREES ; or, Gradual Psalms. Interleaved with Notes from Neale and Littledale's Commentary on the Psalms. *Crown 8vo. 1s. net.*

Bathe.—Works by the Rev. ANTHONY BATHE, M.A.

A LENT WITH JESUS. A Plain Guide for Churchmen. Containing Readings for Lent and Easter Week, and on the Holy Eucharist. *32mo, 1s.*; *or in paper cover*, *6d.*

AN ADVENT WITH JESUS. *32mo, 1s.*, *or in paper cover, 6d.*

WHAT I SHOULD BELIEVE. A Simple Manual of Self-Instruction for Church People. *Small 8vo, limp, 1s.* ; *cloth gilt, 2s.*

Bathe and Buckham.—THE CHRISTIAN'S ROAD BOOK. 2 Parts. By the Rev. ANTHONY BATHE and Rev. F. H. BUCKHAM. Part I. DEVOTIONS. *Sewed, 6d.* ; *limp cloth, 1s.* ; *cloth extra, 1s. 6d.* Part II. READINGS. *Sewed, 1s.* ; *limp cloth, 2s.* ; *cloth extra, 3s.* ; *or complete in one volume, sewed, 1s. 6d.* *limp cloth, 2s. 6d.* ; *cloth extra, 3s. 6d.*

Benson.—Works by the Rev. R. M. BENSON, M.A., Student of Christ Church, Oxford.

THE FOLLOWERS OF THE LAMB : a Series of Meditations, especially intended for Persons living under Religious Vows, and for Seasons of Retreat, etc. *Crown 8vo.* *4s. 6d.*

THE FINAL PASSOVER : A Series of Meditations upon the Passion of our Lord Jesus Christ. *Small 8vo.*

Vol. I.—THE REJECTION. *5s.*
Vol. II.—THE UPPER CHAMBER.
Part I. *5s.*
Part II. *5s.*

Vol. III.—THE DIVINE EXODUS. Parts I. and II. *5s.* each.
Vol. IV.—THE LIFE BEYOND THE GRAVE. *5s.*

THE MAGNIFICAT ; a Series of Meditations upon the Song of the Blessed Virgin Mary. *Small 8vo.* *2s.*

SPIRITUAL READINGS FOR EVERY DAY. *3 vols.* *Small 8vo.* *3s. 6d. each.*
I. ADVENT.   II. CHRISTMAS.   III. EPIPHANY.

BENEDICTUS DOMINUS : A Course of Meditations for Every Day of the Year. Vol. I.—ADVENT TO TRINITY. Vol. II.—TRINITY, SAINTS' DAYS, etc. *Small 8vo.* *3s. 6d. each* ; *or in One Volume, 7s.*

BIBLE TEACHINGS: The Discourse at Capernaum.—St. John vi. *Small 8vo.* *1s.* ; *or with Notes.* *3s. 6d.*

THE WISDOM OF THE SON OF DAVID : An Exposition of the First Nine Chapters of the Book of Proverbs. *Small 8vo.* *3s. 6d.*

THE MANUAL OF INTERCESSORY PRAYER. *Royal 32mo* ; *cloth boards, 1s. 3d.* ; *cloth limp, 9d.*

THE EVANGELIST LIBRARY CATECHISM. Part I. *Small 8vo.* *3s.*

PAROCHIAL MISSIONS. *Small 8vo.* *2s. 6d.*

Bickersteth.—YESTERDAY, TO-DAY, AND FOR EVER:
a Poem in Twelve Books. By EDWARD HENRY BICKERSTETH, D.D.,
late Lord Bishop of Exeter. *18mo. 1s. net. With red borders,*
16mo, 2s. net.

The Crown 8vo Edition (5s.) may still be had.

Bigg.—UNITY IN DIVERSITY: Five Addresses delivered
in the Cathedral Church of Christ, Oxford, during Lent 1899, with
Introduction. By the Rev. CHARLES BIGG, D.D., Regius Professor
of Ecclesiastical History in the University of Oxford. *Crown 8vo. 2s. 6d.*

Blunt.—Works by the Rev. JOHN HENRY BLUNT, D.D.

THE ANNOTATED BOOK OF COMMON PRAYER: Being an
Historical, Ritual, and Theological Commentary on the Devotional
System of the Church of England. *4to. 21s.*

THE COMPENDIOUS EDITION OF THE ANNOTATED BOOK
OF COMMON PRAYER: Forming a concise Commentary on the
Devotional System of the Church of England. *Crown 8vo. 10s. 6d.*

DICTIONARY OF DOCTRINAL AND HISTORICAL THEOLOGY.
By various Writers. *Imperial 8vo. 21s.*

DICTIONARY OF SECTS, HERESIES, ECCLESIASTICAL PAR-
TIES AND SCHOOLS OF RELIGIOUS THOUGHT. By various
Writers. *Imperial 8vo. 21s.*

THE BOOK OF CHURCH LAW. Being an Exposition of the Legal
Rights and Duties of the Parochial Clergy and the Laity of the Church
of England. Revised by the Right Hon. Sir WALTER G. F. PHILLI-
MORE, Bart., D.C.L., and G. EDWARDES JONES, Barrister-at-Law.
Crown 8vo. 8s. net.

A COMPANION TO THE BIBLE: Being a Plain Commentary on
Scripture History, to the end of the Apostolic Age. *Two Vols. small*
8vo. Sold separately. OLD TESTAMEMT. *3s. 6d.* NEW TESTAMENT.
3s. 6d.

HOUSEHOLD THEOLOGY: a Handbook of Religious Information
respecting the Holy Bible, the Prayer Book, the Church, etc., etc.
16mo. Paper cover, 1s. Also the Larger Edition, 3s. 6d.

Body.—Works by the Rev. GEORGE BODY, D.D., Canon of Durham.

THE LIFE OF LOVE. A Course of Lent Lectures. *16mo. 2s. net.*

THE SCHOOL OF CALVARY; or, Laws of Christian Life revealed
from the Cross. *16mo. 2s. net.*

THE LIFE OF JUSTIFICATION. *16mo. 2s. net.*

THE LIFE OF TEMPTATION. *16mo. 2s. net.*

THE PRESENT STATE OF THE FAITHFUL DEPARTED. *Small*
8vo. sewed, 6d. 32mo. cloth, 1s.

Book of Private Prayer, The. For use Twice Daily ; together with the Order for the Administration of the Lord's Supper or Holy Communion. 18*mo. Limp cloth*, 2*s.; Cloth boards*, 2*s.* 6*d.*

Book of Prayer and Daily Texts for English Churchmen. 32*mo.* 1*s. net.*

Boultbee.—A COMMENTARY ON THE THIRTY-NINE ARTICLES OF THE CHURCH OF ENGLAND. By the Rev. T. P. BOULTBEE. *Crown 8vo.* 6*s.*

Bright.—Works by WILLIAM BRIGHT, D.D., late Regius Professor of Ecclesiastical History in the University of Oxford.

THE AGE OF THE FATHERS. Being Chapters in the History of the Church during the Fourth and Fifth Centuries. *Two Vols.* *8vo.* 28*s. net.*

MORALITY IN DOCTRINE. *Crown 8vo.* 7*s.* 6*d.*

SOME ASPECTS OF PRIMITIVE CHURCH LIFE. *Crown 8vo.* 6*s.*

THE ROMAN SEE IN THE EARLY CHURCH : And other Studies in Church History. *Crown 8vo.* 7*s.* 6*d.*

LESSONS FROM THE LIVES OF THREE GREAT FATHERS. St. Athanasius, St. Chrysostom, and St. Augustine. *Crown 8vo.* 6*s.*

THE INCARNATION AS A MOTIVE POWER. *Crown 8vo.* 6*s.*

Bright and Medd.—LIBER PRECUM PUBLICARUM ECCLESIÆ ANGLICANÆ. A GULIELMO BRIGHT, S.T.P., et PETRO GOLDSMITH MEDD, A.M., Latine redditus. *Small 8vo.* 5*s. net.*

Browne.—AN EXPOSITION OF THE THIRTY-NINE ARTICLES, Historical and Doctrinal. By E. H. BROWNE, D.D., sometime Bishop of Winchester. *8vo.* 16*s.*

Campion and Beamont.—THE PRAYER BOOK INTERLEAVED. With Historical Illustrations and Explanatory Notes arranged parallel to the Text. By W. M. CAMPION, D.D., and W. J. BEAMONT, M.A. *Small 8vo.* 7*s.* 6*d.*

Carpenter and Harford-Battersby. — THE HEXATEUCH ACCORDING TO THE REVISED VERSION ARRANGED IN ITS CONSTITUENT DOCUMENTS BY MEMBERS OF THE SOCIETY OF HISTORICAL THEOLOGY, OXFORD. Edited with Introduction, Notes, Marginal References, and Synoptical Tables. By J. ESTLIN CARPENTER, M.A. (Lond.) and G. HARFORD-BATTERSBY, M.A. (Oxon.). *Two vols. 4to.* (*Vol. I. Introduction and Appendices : Vol. II. Text and Notes*). 36*s. net.*

THE COMPOSITION OF THE HEXATEUCH : An Introduction with Select Lists of Words and Phrases. With an Appendix on Laws and Institutions. (*Selected from the above.*) *8vo.* 18*s. net.*

Carter.—Works by, and edited by, the Rev. T. T. CARTER, M.A., late Hon. Canon of Christ Church, Oxford.

SPIRITUAL INSTRUCTIONS. *Crown 8vo.*

THE HOLY EUCHARIST. 3*s.* 6*d.*	OUR LORD'S EARLY LIFE. 3s. 6*d.*
THE DIVINE DISPENSATIONS. 3*s.* 6*d.*	OUR LORD'S ENTRANCE ON HIS
THE LIFE OF GRACE. 3*s.* 6*d.*	MINISTRY. 3*s.* 6*d.*

THE RELIGIOUS LIFE. 3*s.* 6*d.*

A BOOK OF PRIVATE PRAYER FOR MORNING, MID-DAY, AND OTHER TIMES. 18*mo, limp cloth,* 1*s.* ; *cloth, red edges,* 1*s.* 3*d.*

THE DOCTRINE OF THE PRIESTHOOD IN THE CHURCH OF ENGLAND. *Crown 8vo.* 4*s.*

THE DOCTRINE OF CONFESSION IN THE CHURCH OF ENGLAND. *Crown 8vo.* 5*s.*

THE SPIRIT OF WATCHFULNESS AND OTHER SERMONS. *Crown 8vo.* 5*s.*

THE TREASURY OF DEVOTION : a Manual of Prayer for General and Daily Use. Compiled by a Priest.
18*mo.* 2*s.* 6*d.* ; *cloth limp,* 2*s.* Bound with the Book of Common Prayer, 3*s.* 6*d.* Red-Line Edition. *Cloth extra, gilt top.* 18*mo.* 2*s.* 6*d. net.* Large-Type Edition. *Crown 8vo.* 3*s.* 6*d.*

THE WAY OF LIFE : A Book of Prayers and Instruction for the Young at School, with a Preparation for Confirmation. 18*mo.* 1*s.* 6*d.*

THE PATH OF HOLINESS : a First Book of Prayers, with the Service of the Holy Communion, for the Young. Compiled by a Priest. With Illustrations. 16*mo.* 1*s.* 6*d.* ; *cloth limp,* 1*s.*

THE GUIDE TO HEAVEN : a Book of Prayers for every Want. (For the Working Classes.) Compiled by a Priest. 18*mo.* 1*s.* 6*d.*; *cloth limp,* 1*s. Large-Type Edition. Crown 8vo.* 1*s.* 6*d.* ; *cloth limp,* 1*s.*

THE STAR OF CHILDHOOD : a First Book of Prayers and Instruction for Children. Compiled by a Priest. With Illustrations. 16*mo.* 2*s.* 6*d.*

SIMPLE LESSONS; or, Words Easy to be Understood. A Manual of Teaching. I. On the Creed. II. The Ten Commandments. III. The Sacrament. 18*mo.* 3*s.*

MANUAL OF DEVOTION FOR SISTERS OF MERCY. 8 parts in 2 vols. 32mo. 10*s.* Or separately :—Part I. 1*s.* 6*d.* Part II. 1*s.* Part III. 1*s.* Part IV. 2*s.* Part V. 1*s.* Part VI. 1*s.* Part VII. Part VIII. 1*s.* 6*d.*

UNDERCURRENTS OF CHURCH LIFE IN THE EIGHTEENTH CENTURY. *Crown 8vo.* 5*s.*

NICHOLAS FERRAR : his Household and his Friends. With Portrait. *Crown 8vo.* 6*s.*

Coles.—Works by the Rev. V. S. S. COLES, M.A., Principal of the Pusey House, Oxford.

LENTEN MEDITATIONS. 18*mo.* 2*s.* 6*d.*

ADVENT MEDITATIONS ON ISAIAH I.-XII.: together with Outlines of Christmas Meditations on St. John i. 1-12. 18*mo.* 2*s.*

Company, The, of Heaven : Daily Links with the Household of God. Being Selections in Prose and Verse from various Authors. With Autotype Frontispiece. *Crown 8vo.* 3*s.* 6*d. net.*

Conybeare and Howson.—THE LIFE AND EPISTLES OF ST. PAUL. By the Rev. W. J. CONYBEARE, M.A., and the Very Rev. J. S. HOWSON, D.D. With numerous Maps and Illustrations.

LIBRARY EDITION. *Two Vols. 8vo.* 21*s.* STUDENTS' EDITION. *One Vol. Crown 8vo.* 6*s.* POPULAR EDITION. *One Vol. Crown 8vo.* 3*s.* 6*d.*

Creighton.—Works by MANDELL CREIGHTON, D.D., late Lord Bishop of London.

A HISTORY OF THE PAPACY FROM THE GREAT SCHISM TO THE SACK OF ROME (1378-1527). *Six Volumes. Crown 8vo.* 5*s. each net.*

THE CHURCH AND THE NATION : Charges and Addresses. *Crown 8vo.* 5*s. net.*

THOUGHTS ON EDUCATION : Speeches and Sermons. *Crown 8vo.* 5*s. net.*

Day-Hours of the Church of England, The. Newly Revised according to the Prayer Book and the Authorised Translation of the Bible. *Crown 8vo, sewed,* 3*s.* ; *cloth,* 3*s.* 6*d.*

SUPPLEMENT TO THE DAY-HOURS OF THE CHURCH OF ENGLAND, being the Service for certain Holy Days. *Crown 8vo, sewed,* 3*s.* ; *cloth,* 3*s.* 6*d.*

Edersheim.—Works by ALFRED EDERSHEIM, M.A., D.D., Ph.D.

THE LIFE AND TIMES OF JESUS THE MESSIAH. *Two Vols. 8vo.* 12*s. net.*

JESUS THE MESSIAH : being an Abridged Edition of 'The Life and Times of Jesus the Messiah.' *Crown 8vo.* 6*s. net.*

Ellicott.—Works by C. J. ELLICOTT, D.D., Bishop of Gloucester.

A CRITICAL AND GRAMMATICAL COMMENTARY ON ST. PAUL'S EPISTLES. Greek Text, with a Critical and Grammatical Commentary, and a Revised English Translation. *8vo.*

GALATIANS. 8*s.* 6*d.*	PHILIPPIANS, COLOSSIANS, AND
EPHESIANS. 8*s.* 6*d.*	PHILEMON. 10*s.* 6*d.*
PASTORAL EPISTLES. 10*s.* 6*d.*	THESSALONIANS. 7*s.* 6*d.*

HISTORICAL LECTURES ON THE LIFE OF OUR LORD JESUS CHRIST. *8vo.* 12*s.*

English (The) Catholic's Vade Mecum: a Short Manual of General Devotion. Compiled by a PRIEST. 32mo. *limp,* 1s. ; *cloth,* 2s. PRIEST's Edition. 32mo. 1s. 6d.

Epochs of Church History.—Edited by MANDELL CREIGHTON, D.D., late Lord Bishop of London. *Small 8vo.* 2s. 6d. *each.*

THE ENGLISH CHURCH IN OTHER LANDS. By the Rev. H. W. TUCKER, M.A.

THE HISTORY OF THE REFORMATION IN ENGLAND. By the Rev. GEO. G. PERRY, M.A.

THE CHURCH OF THE EARLY FATHERS. By the Rev. ALFRED PLUMMER, D.D.

THE EVANGELICAL REVIVAL IN THE EIGHTEENTH CENTURY. By the Rev. J. H. OVERTON, D.D.

THE UNIVERSITY OF OXFORD. By the Hon. G. C. BRODRICK, D.C.L.

THE UNIVERSITY OF CAMBRIDGE. By J. BASS MULLINGER, M.A.

THE ENGLISH CHURCH IN THE MIDDLE AGES. By the Rev. W. HUNT, M.A.

THE CHURCH AND THE EASTERN EMPIRE. By the Rev. H. F. TOZER, M.A.

THE CHURCH AND THE ROMAN EMPIRE. By the Rev. A. CARR, M.A.

THE CHURCH AND THE PURITANS, 1570-1660. By HENRY OFFLEY WAKEMAN, M.A.

HILDEBRAND AND HIS TIMES. By the Very Rev. W. R. W. STEPHENS, B.D.

THE POPES AND THE HOHENSTAUFEN. By UGO BALZANI.

THE COUNTER REFORMATION. By ADOLPHUS WILLIAM WARD, Litt. D.

WYCLIFFE AND MOVEMENTS FOR REFORM. By REGINALD L. POOLE, M.A.

THE ARIAN CONTROVERSY. By the Rev. Professor H. M. GWATKIN, M.A.

Eucharistic Manual (The). Consisting of Instructions and Devotions for the Holy Sacrament of the Altar. From various sources. 32mo. *cloth gilt, red edges.* 1s. *Cheap Edition, limp cloth.* 9d.

Farrar.—Works by FREDERIC W. FARRAR, D.D., Dean of Canterbury.

TEXTS EXPLAINED ; or, Helps to Understand the New Testament. *Crown 8vo.* 5s. *net.*

THE BIBLE : Its Meaning and Supremacy. *8vo.* 6s. *net.*

ALLEGORIES. With 25 Illustrations by AMELIA BAUERLE. *Crown 8vo. gilt edges.* 2s. 6d. *net.*

Fosbery.—VOICES OF COMFORT. Edited by the Rev. THOMAS VINCENT FOSBERY, M.A., sometime Vicar of St. Giles's, Reading. *Cheap Edition. Small 8vo.* 3s. *net.* *The Larger Edition (7s. 6d.) may still be had.*

Gardner.—A CATECHISM OF CHURCH HISTORY, from the Day of Pentecost until the Present Day. By the Rev. C. E. GARDNER, of the Society of St. John the Evangelist, Cowley. *Crown 8vo, sewed,* 1s. ; *cloth,* 1s. 6d.

Geikie.—Works by J. CUNNINGHAM GEIKIE, D.D., LL.D., late Vicar of St. Martin-at-Palace, Norwich.

THE VICAR AND HIS FRIENDS. *Crown 8vo. 5s. net.*

HOURS WITH THE BIBLE: the Scriptures in the Light of Modern Discovery and Knowledge. *Complete in Twelve Volumes. Crown 8vo.*

OLD TESTAMENT.

CREATION TO THE PATRIARCHS. *With a Map and Illustrations. 5s.*

MOSES TO JUDGES. *With a Map and Illustrations. 5s.*

SAMSON TO SOLOMON. *With a Map and Illustrations. 5s*

REHOBOAM TO HEZEKIAH. *With Illustrations. 5s.*

MANASSEH TO ZEDEKIAH. *With the Contemporary Prophets. With a Map and Illustrations. 5s.*

EXILE TO MALACHI. *With the Contemporary Prophets. With Illustrations. 5s.*

NEW TESTAMENT.

THE GOSPELS. *With a Map and Illustrations. 5s.*

LIFE AND WORDS OF CHRIST. *With Map. 2 vols. 10s.*

LIFE AND EPISTLES OF ST. PAUL. *With Maps and Illustrations. 2 vols. 10s.*

ST. PETER TO REVELATION. *With 29 Illustrations. 5s.*

LIFE AND WORDS OF CHRIST.
Cabinet Edition. With Map. 2 vols. Post 8vo. 10s.
Cheap Edition, without the Notes. 1 vol. 8vo. 6s.
A SHORT LIFE OF CHRIST. *With 34 Illustrations. Crown 8vo. 3s. 6d. ; gilt edges, 4s. 6d.*

Gold Dust: a Collection of Golden Counsels for the Sanctification of Daily Life. Translated and abridged from the French by E.L.E.E. Edited by CHARLOTTE M. YONGE. Parts I. II. III. Small Pocket Volumes. *Cloth, gilt, each* 1s. Parts I. and II. in One Volume. 1s. 6d. Parts I., II., and III. in One Volume. 2s. *net.*

** The two first parts in One Volume, *large type,* 18mo. *cloth, gilt. 2s. net.* Parts I. II. and III. are also supplied, bound in white cloth, with red edges, in box, price 2s. 6d. *net.*

Gore.—Works by the Right Rev. CHARLES GORE, D.D., Lord Bishop of Worcester.
THE CHURCH AND THE MINISTRY. *Fifth Edition, Revised. Crown 8vo. 6s., net.*
ROMAN CATHOLIC CLAIMS. *Crown 8vo. 3s. net.*

Goreh.—THE LIFE OF FATHER GOREH. By C. E. GARDNER, S.S.J.E. Edited, with Preface, by RICHARD MEUX BENSON, M.A., S.S.J.E., Student of Christ Church, Oxford. With Portrait. *Crown 8vo. 5s.*

Great Truths of the Christian Religion. Edited by the Rev. W. U. RICHARDS. *Small 8vo.* 2s.

Hall.—Works by the Right Rev. A. C. A. HALL, D.D., Bishop of Vermont.

CONFIRMATION. *Crown 8vo.* 5s. (*The Oxford Library of Practical Theology.*)

THE VIRGIN MOTHER: Retreat Addresses on the Life of the Blessed Virgin Mary as told in the Gospels. With an appended Essay on the Virgin Birth of our Lord. *Crown 8vo.* 4s. 6d.

CHRIST'S TEMPTATION AND OURS. *Crown 8vo.* 3s. 6d.

Hallowing of Sorrow. By E. R. With a Preface by H. S. HOLLAND, M.A., Canon and Precentor of St. Paul's. *Small 8vo.* 2s.

Hanbury - Tracy. — FAITH AND PROGRESS. Sermons Preached at the Dedication Festival of St. Barnabas' Church, Pimlico, June 10-17, 1900. Edited by the Rev. the Hon. A. HANBURY-TRACY, Vicar of St. Barnabas', Pimlico. With an Introduction by the Rev. T. T. CARTER, M.A. *Crown 8vo.* 4s. 6d. net.

Handbooks for the Clergy. Edited by the Rev. ARTHUR W. ROBINSON, B.D., Vicar of Allhallows Barking by the Tower. *Crown 8vo.* 2s. 6d. net each Volume.

THE PERSONAL LIFE OF THE CLERGY. By the Rev. ARTHUR W. ROBINSON, B.D., Vicar of Allhallows Barking by the Tower.

THE MINISTRY OF CONVERSION. By the Rev. A. J. MASON, D.D., Lady Margaret's Reader in Divinity in the University of Cambridge and Canon of Canterbury.

PATRISTIC STUDY. By the Rev. H. B. SWETE, D.D., Regius Professor of Divinity in the University of Cambridge.

FOREIGN MISSIONS. By the Right Rev. H. H. MONTGOMERY, D.D., formerly Bishop of Tasmania, Secretary of the Society for the Propagation of the Gospel in Foreign Parts.

THE STUDY OF THE GOSPELS. By the Very Rev. J. ARMITAGE ROBINSON, D.D., Dean of Westminster.

A CHRISTIAN APOLOGETIC. By the Very Rev. WILFORD L. ROBINSON, D.D., Dean of Albany, U.S.

₄ *Other Volumes are in preparation.*

Hatch.—THE ORGANIZATION OF THE EARLY CHRISTIAN CHURCHES. Being the Bampton Lectures for 1880. By EDWIN HATCH, M.A., D.D., late Reader in Ecclesiastical History in the University of Oxford. *8vo.* 5s.

A 2

Holland.—Works by the Rev. HENRY SCOTT HOLLAND, M.A., Canon and Precentor of St. Paul's.

GOD'S CITY AND THE COMING OF THE KINGDOM.   *Crown 8vo.   3s. 6d.*

PLEAS AND CLAIMS FOR CHRIST.   *Crown 8vo.   3s. 6d.*

CREED AND CHARACTER : Sermons.   *Crown 8vo.   3s. 6d.*

ON BEHALF OF BELIEF.   Sermons.   *Crown 8vo.   3s. 6d.*

CHRIST OR ECCLESIASTES.   Sermons.   *Crown 8vo.   2s. 6d.*

LOGIC AND LIFE, with other Sermons.   *Crown 8vo.   3s. 6d.*

GOOD FRIDAY.   Being Addresses on the Seven Last Words.   *Small 8vo.   2s.*

Hollings.—Works by the Rev. G. S. HOLLINGS, Mission Priest of the Society of St. John the Evangelist, Cowley, Oxford.

THE HEAVENLY STAIR ; or, A Ladder of the Love of God for Sinners.   *Crown 8vo.   3s. 6d.*

PORTA REGALIS ; or, Considerations on Prayer.   *Crown 8vo. limp cloth, 1s. 6d. net ; cloth boards, 2s. net.*

CONSIDERATIONS ON THE WISDOM OF GOD.   *Crown 8vo.   4s.*

PARADOXES OF THE LOVE OF GOD, especially as they are seen in the way of the Evangelical Counsels.   *Crown 8vo.   4s.*

ONE BORN OF THE SPIRIT ; or, the Unification of our Life in God.   *Crown 8vo.   3s. 6d.*

Hutchings.—Works by the Ven. W. H. HUTCHINGS, M.A. Archdeacon of Cleveland, Canon of York, Rector of Kirby Misperton, and Rural Dean of Malton.

SERMON SKETCHES from some of the Sunday Lessons throughout the Church's Year.   *Vols. I and II.   Crown 8vo.   5s. each.*

THE LIFE OF PRAYER : a Course of Lectures delivered in All Saints' Church, Margaret Street, during Lent.   *Crown 8vo.   4s. 6d.*

THE PERSON AND WORK OF THE HOLY GHOST : a Doctrinal and Devotional Treatise.   *Crown 8vo.   4s. 6d.*

SOME ASPECTS OF THE CROSS.   *Crown 8vo.   4s. 6d.*

THE MYSTERY OF THE TEMPTATION.   Lent Lectures delivered at St. Mary Magdalene, Paddington.   *Crown 8vo.   4s. 6d.*

Hutton.—THE SOUL HERE AND HEREAFTER.   By the Rev. R. E. HUTTON, Chaplain of St. Margaret's, East Grinstead.   *Crown 8vo.   6s.*

Inheritance of the Saints; or, Thoughts on the Communion of Saints and the Life of the World to come. Collected chiefly from English Writers by L. P. With a Preface by the Rev. HENRY SCOTT HOLLAND, M.A. *Ninth Edition. Crown 8vo. 7s. 6d.*

James.—THE VARIETIES OF RELIGIOUS EXPERIENCE: A Study in Human Nature. Being the Gifford Lectures on Natural Religion delivered at Edinburgh in 1901-1902. By WILLIAM JAMES, LLD., etc., Professor of Philosophy at Harvard University. *8vo. 12s. net.*

Jameson.—Works by Mrs. JAMESON.

SACRED AND LEGENDARY ART, containing Legends of the Angels and Archangels, the Evangelists, the Apostles. With 19 Etchings and 187 Woodcuts. *2 vols. 8vo. 20s. net.*

LEGENDS OF THE MONASTIC ORDERS, as represented in the Fine Arts. With 11 Etchings and 88 Woodcuts. *8vo. 10s. net.*

LEGENDS OF THE MADONNA, OR BLESSED VIRGIN MARY. With 27 Etchings and 165 Woodcuts. *8vo. 10s. net.*

THE HISTORY OF OUR LORD, as exemplified in Works of Art. Commenced by the late Mrs. JAMESON ; continued and completed by LADY EASTLAKE. With 31 Etchings and 281 Woodcuts. *2 Vols. 8vo. 20s. net.*

Johnstone.—SONSHIP : Six Lenten Addresses. By the Rev. VERNEY LOVETT JOHNSTONE, M.A., late Assistant Curate of Ilfracombe. With an Introduction by the Rev. V. S. S. COLES, M.A., Principal of the Pusey House, Oxford. *Crown 8vo. 2s.*

Jones.—ENGLAND AND THE HOLY SEE: An Essay towards Reunion. By SPENCER JONES, M.A., Rector of Moreton-in-Marsh. With a Preface by the Right Hon. VISCOUNT HALIFAX. *Crown 8vo. 3s. 6s. net.*

Joy and Strength for the Pilgrim's Day: Selections in Prose and Verse. By the Editor of 'Daily Strength for Daily Needs,' etc. *Small 8vo. 3s. 6d. net.*

Jukes.—Works by ANDREW JUKES.

THE NAMES OF GOD IN HOLY SCRIPTURE : a Revelation of His Nature and Relationships. *Crown 8vo. 4s. 6d.*

THE TYPES OF GENESIS. *Crown 8vo. 7s. 6d.*

THE SECOND DEATH AND THE RESTITUTION OF ALL THINGS. *Crown 8vo. 3s. 6d.*

Kelly.—Works by the Rev. HERBERT H. KELLY, M.A., Director of the Society of the Sacred Mission, Mildenhall, Suffolk.

A HISTORY OF THE CHURCH OF CHRIST. Vol. I. A.D. 29-342. *Crown 8vo.* 3*s.* 6*d. net.* Vol. II. A.D. 324-430. *Crown 8vo.* 3*s.* 6*d. net.*

ENGLAND AND THE CHURCH : Her Calling and its Fulfilment Considered in Relation to the Increase and Efficiency of Her Ministry. *Crown 8vo.* 4*s. net.*

Knox.—PASTORS AND TEACHERS : Six Lectures on Pastoral Theology. By the Right Rev. EDMUND ARBUTHNOTT KNOX, D.D., Bishop of Coventry. With an Introduction by the Right Rev. CHARLES GORE, D.D., Bishop of Worcester. *Crown 8vo.* 5*s. net.*

Knox Little.—Works by W. J. KNOX LITTLE, M.A., Canon Residentiary of Worcester, and Vicar of Hoar Cross.

HOLY MATRIMONY. *Crown 8vo.* 5*s.* (*The Oxford Library of Practical Theology.*)

THE PERFECT LIFE : Sermons. *Crown 8vo.* 7*s.* 6*d.*

THE CHRISTIAN HOME. *Crown 8vo.* 3*s.* 6*d.*

CHARACTERISTICS AND MOTIVES OF THE CHRISTIAN LIFE. Ten Sermons preached in Manchester Cathedral, in Lent and Advent. *Crown 8vo.* 2*s.* 6*d.*

THE MYSTERY OF THE PASSION OF OUR MOST HOLY REDEEMER. *Crown 8vo.* 2*s.* 6*d.*

THE LIGHT OF LIFE. Sermons preached on Various Occasions. *Crown 8vo.* 3*s.* 6*d.*

SUNLIGHT AND SHADOW IN THE CHRISTIAN LIFE. Sermons preached for the most part in America. *Crown 8vo.* 3*s.* 6*d.*

Lear.—Works by, and Edited by, H. L. SIDNEY LEAR.

FOR DAYS AND YEARS. A book containing a Text, Short Reading, and Hymn for Every Day in the Church's Year. 16*mo.* 2*s. net. Also a Cheap Edition*, 32*mo*, 1*s.*; *or cloth gilt*, 1*s.* 6*d.*; *or with red borders*, 2*s. net.*

FIVE MINUTES. Daily Readings of Poetry. 16*mo.* 3*s.* 6*d. Also a Cheap Edition*, 32*mo.* 1*s.*; *or cloth gilt*, 1*s.* 6*d.*

WEARINESS. A Book for the Languid and Lonely. *Large Type. Small 8vo.* 5*s.*

Lear. — Works by, and Edited by, H. L. SIDNEY LEAR.— *continued.*

DEVOTIONAL WORKS. Edited by H. L. SIDNEY LEAR. *New and Uniform Editions. Nine Vols.* 16mo. 2s. net each.

FÉNELON'S SPIRITUAL LETTERS TO MEN.

FÉNELON'S SPIRITUAL LETTERS TO WOMEN.

A SELECTION FROM THE SPIRITUAL LETTERS OF ST. FRANCIS DE SALES. Also *Cheap Edition,* 32mo, 6d. *cloth limp ;* 1s. *cloth boards.*

THE SPIRIT OF ST. FRANCIS DE SALES.

THE HIDDEN LIFE OF THE SOUL.

THE LIGHT OF THE CONSCIENCE. Also *Cheap Edition,* 32mo, 6d. *cloth limp ;* 1s. *cloth boards.*

SELF-RENUNCIATION. From the French.

ST. FRANCIS DE SALES' OF THE LOVE OF GOD.

SELECTIONS FROM PASCAL'S 'THOUGHTS.'

Leighton. — TYPICAL MODERN CONCEPTIONS OF GOD ; or, The Absolute of German Romantic Idealism and of English Evolutionary Agnosticism. With a Constructive Essay. By JOSEPH ALEXANDER LEIGHTON, Professor of Philosophy in Hobart College, U.S. *Crown 8vo.* 3s. 6d. *net.*

Liddon. — Works by HENRY PARRY LIDDON, D.D., D.C.L., LL.D.

SERMONS ON SOME WORDS OF ST. PAUL. *Crown 8vo.* 5s.

SERMONS PREACHED ON SPECIAL OCCASIONS, 1860-1889. *Crown 8vo.* 5s.

CLERICAL LIFE AND WORK : Sermons. *Crown 8vo.* 5s.

ESSAYS AND ADDRESSES : Lectures on Buddhism—Lectures on the Life of St. Paul—Papers on Dante. *Crown 8vo.* 5s.

EXPLANATORY ANALYSIS OF PAUL'S EPISTLE TO THE ROMANS. *8vo.* 14s.

EXPLANATORY ANALYSIS OF ST. PAUL'S FIRST EPISTLE TO TIMOTHY. *8vo.* 7s. 6d.

SERMONS ON OLD TESTAMENT SUBJECTS. *Crown 8vo.* 5s.

SERMONS ON SOME WORDS OF CHRIST. *Crown 8vo.* 5s.

THE DIVINITY OF OUR LORD AND SAVIOUR JESUS CHRIST. Being the Bampton Lectures for 1866. *Crown 8vo.* 5s.

ADVENT IN ST. PAUL'S. *Crown 8vo.* 5s.

CHRISTMASTIDE IN ST. PAUL'S. *Crown 8vo.* 5s.

PASSIONTIDE SERMONS. *Crown 8vo.* 5s.

[continued.

Liddon.—Works by HENRY PARRY LIDDON, D.D., D.C.L., LL.D.—*continued.*

EASTER IN ST. PAUL'S. Sermons bearing chiefly on the Resurrection of our Lord. *Two Vols. Crown 8vo.* 3s. 6d. each. *Cheap Edition in one Volume. Crown 8vo.* 5s.

SERMONS PREACHED BEFORE THE UNIVERSITY OF OXFORD. *Two Vols. Crown 8vo.* 3s. 6d. each. *Cheap Edition in one Volume. Crown 8vo.* 5s.

THE MAGNIFICAT. Sermons in St. Paul's. *Crown 8vo.* 2s. net.

SOME ELEMENTS OF RELIGION. Lent Lectures. *Small 8vo.* 2s. net. [*The Crown 8vo Edition* (5s.) *may still be had.*]

Luckock.—Works by HERBERT MORTIMER LUCKOCK, D.D., Dean of Lichfield.

THE SPECIAL CHARACTERISTICS OF THE FOUR GOSPELS. *Crown 8vo.* 6s.

AFTER DEATH. An Examination of the Testimony of Primitive Times respecting the State of the Faithful Dead, and their Relationship to the Living. *Crown 8vo.* 3s. net.

THE INTERMEDIATE STATE BETWEEN DEATH AND JUDGMENT. Being a Sequel to *After Death. Crown 8vo.* 3s. net.

FOOTPRINTS OF THE SON OF MAN, as traced by St. Mark. Being Eighty Portions for Private Study, Family Reading, and Instruction in Church. *Crown 8vo.* 3s. net.

FOOTPRINTS OF THE APOSTLES, as traced by St. Luke in the Acts. Being Sixty Portions for Private Study, and Instruction in Church. A Sequel to 'Footprints of the Son of Man, as traced by St. Mark.' *Two Vols. Crown 8vo.* 12s.

THE DIVINE LITURGY. Being the Order for Holy Communion, Historically, Doctrinally, and Devotionally set forth, in Fifty Portions. *Crown 8vo.* 3s. net.

STUDIES IN THE HISTORY OF THE BOOK OF COMMON PRAYER. The Anglican Reform—The Puritan Innovations—The Elizabethan Reaction—The Caroline Settlement. With Appendices. *Crown 8vo.* 3s. net.

Lyra Germanica: Hymns for the Sundays and Chief Festivals of the Christian Year. *Complete Edition. Small 8vo.* 5s. *First Series.* 16mo, *with red borders,* 2s. net.

MacColl.—Works by the Rev. MALCOLM MACCOLL, D.D., Canon Residentiary of Ripon.

THE REFORMATION SETTLEMENT: Examined in the Light of History and Law. Tenth Edition, Revised, with a new Preface. *Crown 8vo. 3s. 6d. net.*

CHRISTIANITY IN RELATION TO SCIENCE AND MORALS. *Crown 8vo. 6s.*

LIFE HERE AND HEREAFTER : Sermons. *Crown 8vo. 7s. 6d.*

Marriage Addresses and Marriage Hymns. By the BISHOP OF LONDON, the BISHOP OF ROCHESTER, the BISHOP OF TRURO, the DEAN OF ROCHESTER, the DEAN OF NORWICH, ARCHDEACON SINCLAIR, CANON DUCKWORTH, CANON NEWBOLT, CANON KNOX LITTLE, CANON RAWNSLEY, the Rev. J. LLEWELLYN DAVIES, D.D., the Rev. W. ALLEN WHITWORTH, etc. Edited by the Rev. O. P. WARDELL-YERBURGH, M.A., Vicar of the Abbey Church of St. Mary, Tewkesbury. *Crown 8vo. 5s.*

Mason.—Works by A. J. MASON, D.D., Lady Margaret's Reader in Divinity in the University of Cambridge and Canon of Canterbury.

THE MINISTRY OF CONVERSION. *Crown 8vo. 2s. 6d. net.* (*Handbooks for the Clergy.*)

PURGATORY; THE STATE OF THE FAITHFUL DEAD; INVOCATION OF SAINTS. Three Lectures. *Crown 8vo. 3s. 6d. net.*

THE FAITH OF THE GOSPEL. A Manual of Christian Doctrine. *Crown 8vo. 7s. 6d. Cheap Edition. Crown 8vo. 3s. net.*

THE RELATION OF CONFIRMATION TO BAPTISM. As taught in Holy Scripture and the Fathers. *Crown 8vo. 7s. 6d.*

Maturin.—Works by the Rev. B. W. MATURIN.

SOME PRINCIPLES AND PRACTICES OF THE SPIRITUAL LIFE. *Crown 8vo. 4s. 6d.*

PRACTICAL STUDIES ON THE PARABLES OF OUR LORD. *Crown 8vo. 5s.*

Medd.—THE PRIEST TO THE ALTAR; or, Aids to the Devout Celebration of Holy Communion, chiefly after the Ancient English Use of Sarum. By PETER GOLDSMITH MEDD, M.A., Canon of St. Albans. Fourth Edition, revised and enlarged. *Royal 8vo. 15s.*

Meyrick.—THE DOCTRINE OF THE CHURCH OF England on the Holy Communion Restated as a Guide at the Present Time. By the Rev. F. MEYRICK, M.A. *Crown 8vo. 4s. 6d.*

Monro.—SACRED ALLEGORIES. By Rev. EDWARD MONRO. *Complete Edition in one Volume, with Illustrations. Crown 8vo. 3s. 6d. net.*

Mortimer.—Works by the Rev. A. G. MORTIMER, D.D., Rector of St. Mark's, Philadelphia.

THE CREEDS: An Historical and Doctrinal Exposition of the Apostles', Nicene and Athanasian Creeds. *Crown 8vo.* 5s. *net.*

THE EUCHARISTIC SACRIFICE: An Historical and Theological Investigation of the Sacrificial Conception of the Holy Eucharist in the Christian Church. *Crown 8vo.* 10s. 6d.

CATHOLIC FAITH AND PRACTICE: A Manual of Theology. Two Parts. *Crown 8vo.* Sold Separately. **Part I.** 7s. 6d. **Part II.** 9s.

JESUS AND THE RESURRECTION: Thirty Addresses for Good Friday and Easter. *Crown 8vo.* 5s.

HELPS TO MEDITATION: Sketches for Every Day in the Year.
Vol. I. ADVENT TO TRINITY. *8vo.* 7s. 6d.
Vol. II. TRINITY TO ADVENT. *8vo.* 7s. 6d.

STORIES FROM GENESIS: Sermons for Children. *Crown 8vo.* 4s.

THE LAWS OF HAPPINESS; or, The Beatitudes as teaching our Duty to God, Self, and our Neighbour. *18mo.* 2s.

THE LAWS OF PENITENCE: Addresses on the Words of our Lord from the Cross. *16mo.* 1s. 6d.

SERMONS IN MINIATURE FOR EXTEMPORE PREACHERS: Sketches for Every Sunday and Holy Day of the Christian Year. *Crown 8vo.* 6s.

NOTES ON THE SEVEN PENITENTIAL PSALMS, chiefly from Patristic Sources. *Small 8vo.* 3s. 6d.

THE SEVEN LAST WORDS OF OUR MOST HOLY REDEEMER: with Meditations on some Scenes in His Passion. *Crown 8vo.* 5s.

LEARN OF JESUS CHRIST TO DIE: Addresses on the Words of our Lord from the Cross, taken as teaching the way of Preparation for Death. *16mo.* 2s.

Mozley.—Works by J. B. MOZLEY, D.D., late Canon of Christ Church, and Regius Professor of Divinity at Oxford.

ESSAYS, HISTORICAL AND THEOLOGICAL. *Two Vols.* *8vo.* 24s.

EIGHT LECTURES ON MIRACLES. Being the Bampton Lectures for 1865. *Crown 8vo.* 3s. *net.*

RULING IDEAS IN EARLY AGES AND THEIR RELATION TO OLD TESTAMENT FAITH. *8vo.* 6s.

SERMONS PREACHED BEFORE THE UNIVERSITY OF OXFORD, and on Various Occasions. *Crown 8vo.* 3s. *net.*

SERMONS, PAROCHIAL AND OCCASIONAL. *Crown 8vo.* 3s. *net.*

A REVIEW OF THE BAPTISMAL CONTROVERSY. *Crown 8vo.* 3s. *net.*

Newbolt.—Works by the Rev. W. C. E. NEWBOLT, M.A., Canon and Chancellor of St. Paul's Cathedral.

APOSTLES OF THE LORD: being Six Lectures on Pastoral Theology. *Crown 8vo. 3s. 6d. net.*

RELIGION. *Crown 8vo. 5s.* (*The Oxford Library of Practical Theology.*)

WORDS OF EXHORTATION. Sermons Preached at St. Paul's and elsewhere. *Crown 8vo. 5s. net.*

PENITENCE AND PEACE: being Addresses on the 51st and 23rd Psalms. *Crown 8vo. 2s. net.*

PRIESTLY IDEALS; being a Course of Practical Lectures delivered in St. Paul's Cathedral to 'Our Society' and other Clergy, in Lent, 1898. *Crown 8vo. 3s. 6d.*

PRIESTLY BLEMISHES; or, Some Secret Hindrances to the Realisation of Priestly Ideals. A Sequel. Being a Second Course of Practical Lectures delivered in St. Paul's Cathedral to 'Our Society' and other Clergy in Lent, 1902. *Crown 8vo. 3s. 6d.*

THE GOSPEL OF EXPERIENCE; or, the Witness of Human Life to the truth of Revelation. Being the Boyle Lectures for 1895. *Crown 8vo. 5s.*

COUNSELS OF FAITH AND PRACTICE: being Sermons preached on various occasions. *Crown 8vo. 5s.*

SPECULUM SACERDOTUM; or, the Divine Model of the Priestly Life. *Crown 8vo. 7s. 6d.*

THE FRUIT OF THE SPIRIT. Being Ten Addresses bearing on the Spiritual Life. *Crown 8vo. 2s. net.*

THE MAN OF GOD. *Small 8vo. 1s. 6d.*

THE PRAYER BOOK: Its Voice and Teaching. *Crown 8vo. 2s. net.*

Newman.—Works by JOHN HENRY NEWMAN, B.D., sometime Vicar of St. Mary's, Oxford.

LETTERS AND CORRESPONDENCE OF JOHN HENRY NEWMAN DURING HIS LIFE IN THE ENGLISH CHURCH. With a brief Autobiography. Edited, at Cardinal Newman's request, by ANNE MOZLEY. 2 *vols. Crown 8vo. 7s.*

PAROCHIAL AND PLAIN SERMONS. *Eight Vols. Crown 8vo. 3s. 6d. each.*

SELECTION, ADAPTED TO THE SEASONS OF THE ECCLESIASTICAL YEAR, from the 'Parochial and Plain Sermons.' *Crown 8vo. 3s. 6d.*

FIFTEEN SERMONS PREACHED BEFORE THE UNIVERSITY OF OXFORD. *Crown 8vo. 3s. 6d.*

SERMONS BEARING UPON SUBJECTS OF THE DAY. *Crown 8vo. 3s. 6d.*

LECTURES ON THE DOCTRINE OF JUSTIFICATION. *Crown 8vo. 3s. 6d.*

. *A Complete List of Cardinal Newman's Works can be had on Application.*

Osborne.—Works by EDWARD OSBORNE, Mission Priest of the Society of St. John the Evangelist, Cowley, Oxford.

THE CHILDREN'S SAVIOUR. Instructions to Children on the Life of Our Lord and Saviour Jesus Christ. *Illustrated.* 16mo. 2s. net.

THE SAVIOUR KING. Instructions to Children on Old Testament Types and Illustrations of the Life of Christ. *Illustrated.* 16mo. 2s. net.

THE CHILDREN'S FAITH. Instructions to Children on the Apostles' Creed. *Illustrated.* 16mo. 2s. net.

Ottley.—ASPECTS OF THE OLD TESTAMENT: being the Bampton Lectures for 1897. By ROBERT LAWRENCE OTTLEY, M.A., Vicar of Winterbourne Bassett, Wilts; sometime Principal of the Pusey House. 8vo. 7s. 6d.

Oxford (The) Library of Practical Theology.—Edited by the Rev. W. C. E. NEWBOLT, M.A., Canon and Chancellor of St. Paul's, and the Rev. DARWELL STONE, M.A., Principal of the Missionary College, Dorchester. *Crown 8vo.* 5s. each.

RELIGION. By the Rev. W. C. E. NEWBOLT, M.A., Canon and Chancellor of St. Paul's.

HOLY BAPTISM. By the Rev. DARWELL STONE, M.A., Principal of the Missionary College, Dorchester.

CONFIRMATION. By the Right Rev. A. C. A. HALL, D.D., Bishop of Vermont.

THE HISTORY OF THE BOOK OF COMMON PRAYER. By the Rev. LEIGHTON PULLAN, M.A., Fellow of St. John Baptist's Oxford.

HOLY MATRIMONY. By the Rev. W. J. KNOX LITTLE, M.A., Canon of Worcester.

THE INCARNATION. By the Rev. H. V. S. ECK, M.A., St. Andrew's, Bethnal Green.

FOREIGN MISSIONS. By the Right Rev. E. T. CHURTON, D.D., formerly Bishop of Nassau.

PRAYER. By the Rev. ARTHUR JOHN WORLLEDGE, M.A., Canon and Chancellor of Truro.

SUNDAY. By the Rev. W. B. TREVELYAN, M.A., Vicar of St. Matthew's, Westminster.

THE CHRISTIAN TRADITION. By the Rev. LEIGHTON PULLAN, M.A., Fellow of St. John's College, Oxford.

HOLY ORDERS. By the Rev. A. R. WHITHAM, M.A., Principal of Culham College, Abingdon.   [*In the press.*

DEVOTIONAL BOOKS. By the Rev. CHARLES BODINGTON, Canon and Treasurer of Lichfield.   [*In the press.*

THE BIBLE. By the Rev. DARWELL STONE, M.A., Joint Editor of the Series.   [*In preparation.*

[*continued.*

Oxford (The) Library of Practical Theology.—*continued.*

THE CHURCH CATECHISM THE CHRISTIAN'S MANUAL. By the Rev. W. C. E. NEWBOLT, M.A., Joint Editor of the Series.
[*In preparation.*

RELIGIOUS CEREMONIAL. By the Rev. WALTER HOWARD FRERE, M.A., Superior of the Community of the Resurrection, Examining Chaplain to the Bishop of Rochester. [*In preparation.*

VISITATION OF THE SICK. By the Rev. E. F. RUSSELL, M.A., St. Alban's, Holborn. [*In preparation.*

CHURCH WORK. By the Rev. BERNARD REYNOLDS, M.A., Prebendary of St. Paul's. [*In preparation.*

Paget.—Works by FRANCIS PAGET, D.D., Bishop of Oxford.

CHRIST THE WAY : Four Addresses given at a Meeting of Schoolmasters and others at Haileybury. *Crown 8vo. 1s. 6d. net.*

STUDIES IN THE CHRISTIAN CHARACTER : Sermons. With an Introductory Essay. *Crown 8vo. 4s. net.*

THE SPIRIT OF DISCIPLINE : Sermons. *Crown 8vo. 4s. net.*

FACULTIES AND DIFFICULTIES FOR BELIEF AND DISBELIEF. *Crown 8vo. 4s. net.*

THE HALLOWING OF WORK. Addresses given at Eton, January 16-18, 1888. *Small 8vo. 2s.*

THE REDEMPTION OF WAR : Sermons. *Crown 8vo. 2s. net.*

Passmore.—Works by the Rev. T. H. PASSMORE, M.A.

THE THINGS BEYOND THE TOMB IN A CATHOLIC LIGHT. *Crown 8vo. 2s. 6d. net.*

LEISURABLE STUDIES. *Crown 8vo. 4s. net.*
CONTENTS.—The 'Religious Woman'—Preachments—Silly Ritual—The Tyranny of the Word—The Lectern—The Functions of Ceremonial—Homo Creator—Concerning the Pun—Proverbia.

Percival.—THE INVOCATION OF SAINTS. Treated Theologically and Historically. By HENRY R. PERCIVAL, M.A., D.D. *Crown 8vo. 5s.*

Pocket Manual of Prayers for the Hours, Etc. With the Collects from the Prayer Book. *Royal 32mo. 1s.*

Powell.—CHORALIA : a Handy-Book for Parochial Precentors and Choirmasters. By the Rev. JAMES BADEN POWELL, M.A., Precentor of St. Paul's, Knightsbridge. *Crown 8vo. 4s. 6d. net.*

Practical Reflections. By a CLERGYMAN. With Preface by H. P. LIDDON, D.D., D.C.L., and the LORD BISHOP OF LINCOLN. *Crown 8vo.*

THE BOOK OF GENESIS. 4s. 6d.	THE MINOR PROPHETS. 4s. 6d.
THE PSALMS. 5s.	THE HOLY GOSPELS. 4s. 6d.
ISAIAH. 4s. 6d.	ACTS TO REVELATION. 6s.

Preparatio; or, Notes of Preparation for Holy Communion, founded on the Collect, Epistle, and Gospel for Every Sunday in the Year. With Preface by the Rev. GEORGE CONGREVE, S.S.J.E. *Crown 8vo. 6s. net.*

Priest's Prayer Book (The). Containing Private Prayers and Intercessions; Occasional, School, and Parochial Offices; Offices for the Visitation of the Sick, with Notes, Readings, Collects, Hymns, Litanies, etc. With a brief Pontifical. By the late Rev. R. F. LITTLEDALE, LL.D., D.C.L., and Rev. J. EDWARD VAUX, M.A., F.S.A. *Post 8vo. 6s. 6d.*

Pullan.—Works by the Rev. LEIGHTON PULLAN, M.A., Fellow of St. John Baptist's College.

LECTURES ON RELIGION. *Crown 8vo. 6s.*

THE HISTORY OF THE BOOK OF COMMON PRAYER. *Crown 8vo. 5s.* (*The Oxford Library of Practical Theology.*)

Puller.—THE PRIMITIVE SAINTS AND THE SEE OF ROME. By F. W. PULLER, of the Society of St. John the Evangelist, Cowley. With an Introduction by EDWARD, LORD BISHOP OF LINCOLN. Third Edition, Revised and Enlarged. *8vo. 16s. net.*

Pusey.—Works by the Rev. E. B. PUSEY, D.D.

PRIVATE PRAYERS. With Preface by H. P. LIDDON, D.D., late Chancellor and Canon of St. Paul's. *Royal 32mo. 1s.*

SPIRITUAL LETTERS OF EDWARD BOUVERIE PUSEY, D.D. Edited and prepared for publication by the Rev. J. O. JOHNSTON, M.A., Principal of the Theological College, Cuddesdon; and the Rev. W. C. E. NEWBOLT, M.A., Canon and Chancellor of St. Paul's. New and cheaper Edition. With Index. *Crown 8vo. 5s. net.*

Pusey.—THE STORY OF THE LIFE OF DR. PUSEY. By the Author of 'Charles Lowder.' With Frontispiece. *Crown 8vo. 7s. 6d. net.*

Randolph.—Works by B. W. RANDOLPH, D.D., Principal of the Theological College and Hon. Canon of Ely.

THE EXAMPLE OF THE PASSION: being Addresses given in St. Paul's Cathedral at the Mid-Day Service on Monday, Tuesday, Wednesday, and Thursday in Holy Week, and at the Three Hours' Service on Good Friday, 1897. *Small 8vo. 2s. net.*

MEDITATIONS ON THE OLD TESTAMENT for Every Day in the Year. *Crown 8vo. 6s.*

THE THRESHOLD OF THE SANCTUARY: being Short Chapters on the Inner Preparation for the Priesthood. *Crown 8vo. 3s. 6d.*

RIVINGTON'S DEVOTIONAL SERIES.

16mo, Red Borders and gilt edges. Each 2s. net.

BICKERSTETH'S YESTERDAY, TO-DAY, AND FOR EVER. *Gilt edges.*

CHILCOT'S TREATISE ON EVIL THOUGHTS. *Red edges.*

THE CHRISTIAN YEAR. *Gilt edges.*

HERBERT'S POEMS AND PROVERBS. *Gilt edges.*

THOMAS À KEMPIS' OF THE IMITA-TION OF CHRIST. *Gilt edges.*

LEAR'S (H. L. SIDNEY) FOR DAYS AND YEARS. *Gilt edges.*

LYRA APOSTOLICA. POEMS BY J. W. BOWDEN, R. H. FROUDE, J. KEBLE, J. H. NEWMAN, R. I. WILBERFORCE, AND I. WILLIAMS; and a Preface by CARDINAL NEWMAN. *Gilt edges.*

FRANCIS DE SALES' (ST.) THE DEVOUT LIFE. *Gilt edges.*

WILSON'S THE LORD'S SUPPER. *Red edges.*

*TAYLOR'S (JEREMY) HOLY LIVING. *Red edges.*

*————— HOLY DYING. *Red edges.*

SCUDAMORE'S STEPS TO THE ALTAR.. *Gilt edges*

LYRA GERMANICA: HYMNS FOR THE SUNDAYS AND CHIEF FESTIVALS OF THE CHRISTIAN YEAR. *First Series. Gilt edges.*

LAW'S TREATISE ON CHRISTIAN PERFECTION. Edited by L. H. M. SOULSBY. *Gilt edges.*

CHRIST AND HIS CROSS: SELEC-TIONS FROM SAMUEL RUTHER-FORD'S LETTERS. Edited by L. H. M. SOULSBY. *Gilt edges.*

* These two in one Volume. 5s.

18mo, without Red Borders. Each 1s. net.

BICKERSTETH'S YESTERDAY, TO-DAY, AND FOR EVER.

THE CHRISTIAN YEAR.

THOMAS À KEMPIS' OF THE IMITA-TION OF CHRIST.

HERBERT'S POEMS AND PROVERBS.

SCUDAMORE'S STEPS TO THE ALTAR.

WILSON'S THE LORD'S SUPPER.

FRANCIS DE SALES' (ST.) THE DEVOUT LIFE.

*TAYLOR'S (JEREMY) HOLY LIVING.

*————— HOLY DYING.

* These two in one Volume. 2s. 6d.

Robbins.—Works by WILFORD L. ROBBINS, D.D., Dean of the Cathedral of All Saints', Albany, U.S.

AN ESSAY TOWARD FAITH. *Small 8vo. 3s. net.*

A CHRISTIAN APOLOGETIC. *Crown 8vo. 2s. 6d. net. (Handbooks for the Clergy.)*

Robinson.—Works by the Rev. C. H. ROBINSON, M.A., Editorial Secretary to the S.P.G. and Canon of Ripon.

STUDIES IN THE CHARACTER OF CHRIST. *Crown 8vo. 3s. 6d.*

HUMAN NATURE A REVELATION OF THE DIVINE: a Sequel to 'Studies in the Character of Christ.' *Crown 8vo. 6s. net.*

Romanes.—THOUGHTS ON THE COLLECTS FOR THE TRINITY SEASON. By ETHEL ROMANES, Author of 'The Life and Letters of George John Romanes.' With a Preface by the Right Rev. the LORD BISHOP OF LONDON. *18mo. 2s. 6d. ; gilt edges. 3s. 6d.*

Sanday.—Works by W. SANDAY, D.D., LL.D., Lady Margaret Professor of Divinity and Canon of Christ Church, Oxford.

DIFFERENT CONCEPTIONS OF PRIESTHOOD AND SACRI-FICE : a Report of a Conference held at Oxford, December 13 and 14, 1899. Edited by W. SANDAY, D.D. *8vo. 7s. 6d.*

INSPIRATION : Eight Lectures on the Early History and Origin of the Doctrine of Biblical Inspiration. Being the Bampton Lectures for 1893. *8vo. 7s. 6d.*

Sanders.—FÉNELON: HIS FRIENDS AND HIS ENEMIES, 1651-1715. By E. K. SANDERS. With Portrait. *8vo. 10s. 6d. net.*

Scudamore.—STEPS TO THE ALTAR: a Manual of Devotion for the Blessed Eucharist. By the Rev. W. E. SCUDAMORE, M.A. *Royal 32mo. 1s.*

On toned paper, and rubricated, 2s.: The same, with Collects, Epistles, and Gospels, 2s. 6d. ; 18mo, 1s. net; Demy 18mo, cloth, large type, 1s. 3d.; 16mo, with red borders, 2s. net; Imperial 32mo, limp cloth, 6d.

Simpson.—Works by the Rev. W. J. SPARROW SIMPSON, M.A., Vicar of St. Mark's, Regent's Park.

THE CHURCH AND THE BIBLE. *Crown 8vo. 3s. 6d.*

THE CLAIMS OF JESUS CHRIST : Lent Lectures. *Crown 8vo. 3s.*

Skrine.—PASTOR AGNORUM : a Schoolmaster's After-thoughts. By JOHN HUNTLEY SKRINE, Warden of Glenalmond, Author of 'A Memory of Edward Thring, etc. Crown 8vo. *5s. net.*

Soulsby.—SUGGESTIONS ON PRAYER. By LUCY H. M. SOULSBY. *18mo, sewed, 1s. net. ; cloth, 1s. 6d. net.*

Stone.—Works by the Rev. DARWELL STONE, M.A., Principal of Dorchester Missionary College.

OUTLINES OF MEDITATIONS FOR USE IN RETREAT. *Crown 8vo. 2s. 6d. net.*

CHRIST AND HUMAN LIFE: Lectures delivered in St. Paul's Cathedral in January 1901 ; together with a Sermon on 'The Father-hood of God.' *Crown 8vo. 2s. 6d. net.*

OUTLINES OF CHRISTIAN DOGMA. *Crown 8vo. 7s. 6d.*

HOLY BAPTISM. *Crown 8vo. 5s. (The Oxford Library of Practical Theology.)*

Strange.—INSTRUCTIONS ON THE REVELATION OF ST. JOHN THE DIVINE: Being an attempt to make this book more intelligible to the ordinary reader and so to encourage the study of it. By Rev. CRESSWELL STRANGE, M.A., Vicar of Edgbaston, and Honorary Canon of Worcester. *Crown 8vo. 6s.*

Strong.—CHRISTIAN ETHICS : being the Bampton Lectures for 1895. By THOMAS B. STRONG, D.D., Dean of Christ Church, Oxford. *8vo. 7s. 6d.*

Stubbs.—ORDINATION ADDRESSES. By the Right Rev. W. STUBBS, D.D., late Lord Bishop of Oxford. Edited by the Rev. E. E. HOLMES, formerly Domestic Chaplain to the Bishop ; Hon. Canon of Christ Church, Oxford. With Photogravure Portrait. *Crown 8vo. 6s. net.*

Waggett.—THE AGE OF DECISION. By P. N. WAGGETT, M.A., of the Society of St. John the Evangelist, Cowley St. John, Oxford. *Crown 8vo. 2s. 6d. net.*

Williams.—Works by the Rev. ISAAC WILLIAMS, B.D.

A DEVOTIONAL COMMENTARY ON THE GOSPEL NARRATIVE. *Eight Vols. Crown 8vo. 5s. each.*

THOUGHTS ON THE STUDY OF THE HOLY GOSPELS.	OUR LORD'S MINISTRY (Second Year).
A HARMONY OF THE FOUR EVANGELISTS.	OUR LORD'S MINISTRY (Third Year).
	THE HOLY WEEK.
OUR LORD'S NATIVITY.	OUR LORD'S PASSION.
	OUR LORD'S RESURRECTION.

FEMALE CHARACTERS OF HOLY SCRIPTURE. A Series of Sermons. *Crown 8vo. 5s.*

THE CHARACTERS OF THE OLD TESTAMENT. *Crown 8vo. 5s.*

THE APOCALYPSE. With Notes and Reflections. *Crown 8vo. 5s.*

SERMONS ON THE EPISTLES AND GOSPELS FOR THE SUNDAYS AND HOLY DAYS. *Two Vols. Crown 8vo. 5s. each.*

PLAIN SERMONS ON CATECHISM. *Two Vols. Cr. 8vo. 5s. each.*

Wirgman.—THE DOCTRINE OF CONFIRMATION. By A. THEODORE WIRGMAN, D.D., D.C.L., Canon of Grahamstown, and Vice-Provost of St. Mary's Collegiate Church, Port Elizabeth, South Africa. *Crown 8vo. 3s. 6d.*

Wordsworth.—Works by CHRISTOPHER WORDSWORTH, D.D., sometime Bishop of Lincoln.

THE HOLY BIBLE (the Old Testament). With Notes, Introductions, and Index. *Imperial 8vo.*
Vol. I. THE PENTATEUCH. 25s. Vol. II. JOSHUA TO SAMUEL. 15s. Vol. III. KINGS to ESTHER. 15s. Vol. IV. JOB TO SONG OF SOLOMON. 25s. Vol. V. ISAIAH TO EZEKIEL. 25s. Vol. VI. DANIEL, MINOR PROPHETS, and Index. 15s.
Also supplied in 13 *Parts. Sold separately.*

THE NEW TESTAMENT, in the Original Greek. With Notes, Introductions, and Indices. *Imperial 8vo.*
Vol. I. GOSPELS AND ACTS OF THE APOSTLES. 23s. Vol. II. EPISTLES, APOCALYPSE, and Indices. 37s.
Also supplied in 4 *Parts. Sold separately.*

CHURCH HISTORY TO A.D. 451. *Four Vols. Crown 8vo.*
Vol. I. TO THE COUNCIL OF NICÆA, A.D. 325. 8s. 6d. Vol. II. FROM THE COUNCIL OF NICÆA TO THAT OF CONSTANTINOPLE. 6s. Vol. III. CONTINUATION. 6s. Vol. IV. CONCLUSION, TO THE COUNCIL OF CHALCEDON, A.D. 451. 6s.

THEOPHILUS ANGLICANUS: a Manual of Instruction on the Church and the Anglican Branch of it. *12mo.* 2s. 6d.

ELEMENTS OF INSTRUCTION ON THE CHURCH. *16mo.* 1s. *cloth.* 6d. *sewed.*

THE HOLY YEAR: Original Hymns. *16mo.* 2s. 6d. *and* 1s. *Limp,* 6d.
,,   ,,   With Music. Edited by W. H. MONK. *Square 8vo.* 4s. 6d.

ON THE INTERMEDIATE STATE OF THE SOUL AFTER DEATH. *32mo.* 1s.

Wordsworth.—Works by JOHN WORDSWORTH, D.D., Lord Bishop of Salisbury.

THE MINISTRY OF GRACE: Studies in Early Church History, with reference to Present Problems. *8vo.*

THE HOLY COMMUNION: Four Visitation Addresses. 1891. *Crown 8vo.* 3s. 6d.

THE ONE RELIGION: Truth, Holiness, and Peace desired by the Nations, and revealed by Jesus Christ. Eight Lectures delivered before the University of Oxford in 1881. *Crown 8vo.* 7s. 6d.

UNIVERSITY SERMONS ON GOSPEL SUBJECTS. *Sm. 8vo.* 2s. 6d.

PRAYERS FOR USE IN COLLEGE. *16mo.* 1s.

10,000/11/02.

Edinburgh: Printed by T. and A. CONSTABLE.

Ingram Content Group UK Ltd.
Milton Keynes UK
UKHW021448090323
418300UK00007B/715